T E A C H

GW00362290

Shirley Baldwin
and Sarah Boas

Hodder & Stoughton

A MEMBER OF THE HODDER HEADLINE GROUP

ACKNOWLEDGMENTS

The authors and publishers are grateful to the following for supplying
photographs:

Barnaby's Picture Library: (pp. 9, 21, 30, 59)
J. Allan Cash Ltd: (Cover, pp. 1, 6, 12, 18, 23, 24, 26, 34, 38, 40, 50, 57,
62, 67, 71)
D.J. Fox: (pp. 30, 42, 55)
Spanish Tourist Board Picture Library: (pp. 6, 53)
Life File, Juliet Highet: (p. 7); Nicola Wells (p. 16);
Emma Lee (pp. 19, 47)

Long-renowned as the authoritative source for self-guided
learning – with more than 30 million copies sold worldwide –
the *Teach Yourself* series includes over 200 titles in the fields
of languages, crafts, hobbies, sports, and other leisure activities.

British Library Cataloguing in Publication Data
Baldwin, Shirley
  Holiday Spanish
  I. Title II. Boas, Sarah
  468.3421
ISBN 0 340 63118 X

First published 1988 as *Spanish in a week*
Re-published 1995 as *Teach Yourself Holiday Spanish*
Impression number   10 9 8 7 6 5 4 3 2 1
Year   1999 1998 1997 1996 1995

Typeset by Transet Ltd, Coventry, Warwickshire.
Printed in Great Britain by Butler & Tanner Ltd, Frome and London, for
Hodder & Stoughton Educational, a division of Hodder Headline Plc,
338 Euston Road, London NW1 3BH.

CONTENTS

INTRODUCTION

Holiday Spanish is a short course which will equip you to deal with everyday situations when you visit Spain: shopping, eating out, asking for directions, changing money, using the phone and so on.

The course is divided into 7 units, each corresponding to a day in the life of Carmen (a journalist) and her two teenage children during their week in Spain. Each unit begins with a dialogue, which introduces the essential language items in context. Key phrases are highlighted in the dialogues, and the phrasebook section which follows lists these and other useful phrases and tells you what they are in English.

Within the units there are also short information sections in English on the topics covered, sections giving basic grammatical explanations, and a number of follow-up activities designed to be useful as well as fun. Answers can be checked in a key at the back of the book.

Pronunciation

1   Pronounce each part of every word; Spanish sounds very much as it is written.
2   Emphasise the last syllable of every word which ends in a consonant other than **n** or **s**.
3   Emphasise the second-to-last syllable of every word which ends with a vowel or **n** or **s**. (Exceptions to these rules carry a written accent.)

Vowels: nearer to Scottish pronunciation than to southern English:

a as *u* in *humbug*; l**a**, m**a**m**á**

e as in *next*; **e**st**e**, s**e**ñor

i as *ee* in *meek*; m**i**, mar**i**do
   Before another vowel:
   like **y**; d**i**a [dee**y**a], b**i**en

o as in *moss*; c**o**che, c**o**m**o**

u as *oo* in *moose*; l**u**nes, m**u**cho
   Before another vowel or **y**:
   like **w**: b**u**eno [b**w**ehno], m**u**y
   [m**w**ee]
   After **q** and in **gue/gui**:
   u is silent; aq**u**í [akee], seg**u**ida

Consonants: similar to English but with the following exceptions:

b Between vowels:
   almost **v**; be**b**ida, tra**b**ajo

c Before **a, o, u**:
   like *kilo*; **c**omo, **c**oche
   Before **e, i**:
   like *thanks*; gra**c**ias, ha**c**e

ch like *chair*; mu**ch**o, **ch**ico

d Between vowels & at end of words:
   almost like *th*; segui**d**a, verda**d**

g Before **a, o, u**: like *gap*; **g**usto
   Before **e, i**: like *loch*; **g**eneral

h always silent **h**ija, **h**otel

j like *loch*; hi**j**a, a**j**o

ll like *bullion*; **ll**amo [**ly**ahmo]

ñ like *onion*; se**ñ**or, se**ñ**ora

qu like *kilo*; **qu**e, a**qu**í

r always sounded, sometimes
   rolled: ve**r**dad

rr strongly rolled: co**rr**eos,
   co**rr**ida

s like *sun*; **s**í, **s**oy

v mixture of **b** and **v**; **v**amos

z like *thank*; pla**z**a, **z**apato

1 ARRIVING IN SPAIN

INTRODUCING YOURSELF

Arrival   When arriving in Spain you will find customs (**Aduana**) and passport procedures standard and easy to follow, as most information is given in English as well as Spanish.

mucho gusto/pleased to meet you

Carmen Roberts, a Spanish journalist working in London, has been sent to Madrid to research a story. She is with her husband, Tom and their two children, Luisa and Miguel. The family is met in Madrid by Andrés Valbuena, a fellow journalist.

Andrés:	**Hola, Buenos días. ¿Es usted la señora Roberts, por favor?**
Carmen:	**Sí, soy** Carmen Roberts. **¿Cómo se llama usted?**
Andrés:	**Me llamo** Andrés Valbuena. **Encantado**, señora Roberts.
Carmen:	**Encantada**. Le presento a mi marido, Tom.
Andrés:	**Mucho gusto, señor.**
Carmen:	**Esta es mi hija,** Luisa, y este ... (sees Miguel looking at some magazines) es mi hijo. ¡Miguel, venga! Que nos vamos con el señor Valbuena.

1 ARRIVING IN SPAIN

On the way to the newspaper office Luisa and Miguel are dropped off at their aunt's flat. Luisa is greeted by Juan, her 19-year-old Spanish cousin.

Juan:	**¡Hola! ¿Qué tal,** Luisa?
Luisa:	**Muy bien, ¿y tú, cómo estás?**
Juan:	Pues, **bien, gracias.** ¡Hola, Miguel! ¿Qué tal?
Miguel:	Bien, gracias.
Juan:	Dame tus maletas. (He picks up the suitcases)
Luisa:	**Gracias,** primo, eres muy amable.
Juan:	**De nada.**
Luisa:	Y tu madre, ¿cómo está?
Juan:	Mi madre está bien. (Calls) ¡Mamá! Aquí están Luisa y Miguel.
Pilar:	¡Qué bien, Luisa y Miguel!

Saying hello

Hola. Buenos días	Hello. Good morning
Buenas tardes	Good afternoon, good evening
Buenas noches	Good evening, good night

▶ ▶ ▶   **Addressing people in Spanish** You should address a man as **señor** (Mr), a woman as **señora** (Mrs), and a girl or young unmarried woman as **señorita** (Miss). It is normal to shake hands both when meeting someone for the first time and also when saying Hello or Goodbye to a friend or acquaintance. Note that there is a formal and informal way of saying 'you'. Use the formal **usted** form (the third person of the verb) until you know somebody well, then change to the **tú** form (the second person). In the family and among friends and younger people the informal form is very frequently used.

Meeting people

¿Cómo se llama usted?	What's your name? (formal)
¿Cómo te llamas?	What's your name? (informal)
Me llamo .../Soy	My name is .../I am
¿Cómo se llama?	What's his/her name?
Se llama ...	His/her name is ...
¿Es usted la señora Valbuena?	Are you Mrs Valbuena?
Este es ... (mi hijo)	This is ... (my son)
Esta es ... (mi hija)	This is ... (my daughter)
Le presento a ...	May I introduce you to ... (formal)
... mi esposa, mi marido	... my wife, my husband
... mi amigo, mi amiga	... my friend
Encantado/Encantada ...	Pleased ...
...de conocerle	... to meet you
Mucho gusto/Tanto gusto	Pleased to meet you

1 ARRIVING IN SPAIN

Asking how someone is

¿Cómo está usted?	How are you (formal)
Muy bien, gracias, ¿y usted?	Very well, thank you, and you?
¿Cómo estás? ¿Qué tal?	How are you? (less formal)
¿Qué hay?	How are things? How's it going?
Muy bien, ¿y tú?	Fine (thanks), and you?
Bien	O.K
¿Cómo está?	How is he/she?
Está bien	He/she is well

Yes and No

Sí/No   Yes/No

Saying please and thank you

Por favor/Gracias	Please/Thank you
Muchas gracias	Thank you very much
Eres muy amable	You are very kind (informal)
De nada/No hay de qué	You're welcome/Don't mention it

OTHER USEFUL PHRASES

¡Venga!	Come here!
Vamos en coche	We are going by car
con el señor Valbuena	with Mr Valbuena
Dame tu maleta	Give me your suitcase
Tu madre/Mi madre	Your mother/My mother
¡Qué bien!	How nice!

the way it works

People and things

In Spanish words for both people and things are said to be either masculine or feminine. The word for 'the' is:
el for a masculine word: **el** señor (man), **el** coche (car):
la for a feminine word: **la** señora (lady), **la** maleta (suitcase).
Most words ending in -o are masculine (**el** hij**o** = son, **el** marido = husband) and most words ending in -a are feminine (**la** esposa = wife, **la** maleta = suitcase). But there are several other endings and it is a good idea to learn each word together with el or la, e.g. el coche = car (-e is usually masculine). Don't worry if you get it wrong. You'll usually be understood!

To make a word plural

el becomes **los**, and la becomes **las**. The ending of the word changes: add -s to words ending in a vowel and -es to words ending in a consonant. e.g. **las** maleta**s** (the suitcases), **los** señor**es** (the men).

1 ARRIVING IN SPAIN

Who are you?/What are you?

Soy Carmen Roberts	I am Carmen Roberts
Eres muy amable	You are very kind
¿**Es** usted el señor Valbuena?	Are you Mr Valbuena?

You will see that there are two verbs in Spanish meaning 'to be'. The one we meet first is **ser**. Here is the pattern of its present tense:

singular			*plural*		
(yo)	**soy**	I am	(nosotros)	**somos**	we are
(tú)	**eres**	you are (informal)	(vosotros)	**sois**	you are
(él/ella)	**es**	he/she/it is	(ellos/ellas)	**son**	they are
(usted)	**es**	you are (formal)	(ustedes)	**son**	you are (formal)

Use this verb for saying who you are and for describing permanent qualities.

Subject pronouns

Yo (I), **tú**, **usted** (you), **él** (he) etc. are *subject pronouns*. Because the ending of the verb shows who is the subject, you do not normally need to use these except to avoid ambiguity or to emphasise the subject.

How are you?/Where are you?

¿**Cómo** estás?	How are you?
Estoy muy bien	I am very well

The second verb meaning 'to be' is **estar**.
Here is the pattern of its endings:

estoy	I am	**estamos**	we are
estás	you are	**estáis**	you are
está	he/she is	**están**	they are
está	you are (formal)	**están**	you are (formal)

Use this verb for asking how someone is and for talking about where something or somebody is:

Aquí **está** Luisa	Here is Luisa
¿Dónde **están?**	Where are they?

My/your/his

There are several examples of these possessive adjectives in the Dialogues: mi esposa, mi hijo, mi hija, tus maletas, tu madre. The full list is as follows:

mi/mis	my	**nuestro(s)/nuestra(s)**	our
tu/tus	your (informal)	**vuestro(s)/vuestra(s)**	your (informal) (when
su/sus	your (formal); his/her/		talking to more than one
	its/their		person)

Note: The possessive adjective agrees in gender and number *with the word it accompanies*, not with the possessor.

Exclamations

¡Hola! Hello!   **¡Venga!** Come here!   **¡Qué bien!** How nice!

In written Spanish you always put an inverted exclamation mark at the beginning as well as the normal one at the end.

1 ARRIVING IN SPAIN

Asking questions and saying No

Asking a question is very simple. There are several alternative methods:

Question: ¿Es usted la señora Roberts? (subject pronoun after verb)
  ¿Usted es la señora Roberts? (same word order, rising intonation)
  Usted es la señora Roberts, **¿verdad?** (no change of word order but
  add **¿verdad?** or **¿no?** = 'isn't it? etc).
Other questions start with words such as **¿Dónde?** (where?) or **¿Cuándo?** (when?).

In written Spanish you always put an inverted question-mark at the beginning of
every question as well as the normal one at the end.
Negative statement Insert **no** immediately before the verb.
No, **no** soy Carmen Roberts   I am not Carmen Roberts

things to do

.1 Carmen is meeting a lot of people. Some of them she knows already; e.g.:
José Machado, elderly business colleague of her husband:
Buenos días, señor. [She asks him how he is]
¿Cómo está usted?

1 Mrs Valbuena, wife of the lawyer:
  [She says good morning and asks her how she is]
2 Mr Gómez, business contact:
  [She says good afternoon, and asks him how he is]
3 Luis Ferrer, an old friend:
  [She says hello and asks him how he is]
  He says: Estoy muy bien, gracias, ¿y tú, cómo estás?
  [She says that she is well]
4 Mari-Carmen Alfonso, your daughter's friend:
  [She says hello, good afternoon, and asks how things are]

.2 Annie Rogers has arrived with her brother (**su hermano**) for a visit to a
Spanish family. What does she say to the customs officer?

Aduanero: Su pasaporte, por favor. ¿Es usted la señorita Rogers?
Annie: ....
Aduanero: Este es su hermano, ¿verdad?
Annie: ....
Aduanero: ¿Es esta su maleta?
Annie: ....
Aduanero: Y ¿esta es la maleta de su hermano?
Annie: ....
Aduanero: Muy bien, señorita, gracias.

.3 Can you say what question was asked to which the answer is the
following?
1 Sí, soy la señora Barillo.   4 Estoy muy bien, gracias.
2 No, no es mi maleta.   5 Mi hermana se llama María Teresa.
3 Está en la oficina.

1 ARRIVING IN SPAIN

YOUR HOLIDAY HOME

¿cómo es tu casa?/what's your house like?

Juan plans to take Luisa and Juan to his holiday house near Santander.

Luisa:	**¿Dónde está tu casa?**
Juan:	**Está cerca de Santander**
Luisa:	¿Cómo es la casa? **¿Es grande?**
Juan:	**No, es bastante pequeña**. Tiene dos dormitorios, un cuarto de estar, un comedor, una cocina moderna, un cuarto de baño, y también tiene una terraza y un jardín.
Luisa:	¿Está cerca del mar?
Juan:	Sí, está muy cerca y hay una vista maravillosa de la playa.
Luisa:	¡Estupendo! **¿Cuándo vamos?**
Juan:	Pues, **¿vamos el miércoles?**
Luisa:	De acuerdo. El miércoles está bien. ¿Vamos en tren?
Juan:	Sí. Vamos en tren a Santander.

Your holiday house

¿Dónde está tu casa?	Where is your house?
Está cerca de ...	It's near ...
¿Cómo es la casa/el piso?	What's the house/flat like?
grande, pequeño/a	big, small
Tiene	It has
dos dormitorios	two bedrooms
un cuarto de estar	a living-room
un comedor	a dining-room

1 BAR AND SOCIAL

una cocina moderna	a modern kitchen
un cuarto de baño	a bathroom
una terraza, un jardín	a terrace, a garden
Está muy cerca del mar	It's very near the sea
Hay una vista maravillosa	There is a wonderful view
de la playa	of the beach

Days of the week (*see page 79 for the complete list*)

¿Cuándo vamos?	When shall we go?
Vamos el miércoles	We'll go on Wednesday
El miércoles está bien	Wednesday is fine

OTHER USEFUL PHRASES

muy	very	también	too, also	De acuerdo	Agreed
bastante	quite, enough	¡Estupendo!	Great!	Vamos en tren	We'll go by train

BUYING A DRINK OR SNACK

Spanish bars Spanish bars are crowded and friendly places and offer a wide variety of drinks and food. You can choose to stand at the counter (**la barra**) or sit at a table, or sometimes on the terrace (**terraza**), where you can watch the world go by but will pay a bit more. Although service will have been included, it is customary to give an extra tip (5% – 10%) or at least to give some small change, if you are pleased with the service.

Many bars serve food as well. Often you will find rows of small dishes of appetizers (**tapas**) containing meat, fish or salads laid out on the counter. Larger portions are called **raciones**, and are often substantial enough to be a meal in themselves.

7

1 BAR AND SOCIAL

vamos a tomar una copa/let's have a drink

Before supper the family decide to pay a visit to a nearby bar.

Camarero:	Buenas tardes, señores. ¿Qué van a tomar?
Carmen:	Miguel, tú ¿qué tomas?
Miguel:	**Una coca-cola, por favor**.
Carmen:	**Y para mí un vermut**. Con hielo y limón, por favor. ¿Y tú, Luisa?
Luisa:	**Quiero** un zumo de naranja, por favor.
Camarero:	Sí, señorita.
Tom:	Yo quiero un tinto, por favor. favor.
Camarero:	Muy bien, señores. ¿Quieren algo para comer?
Carmen:	**¿Qué tapas hay?**
Camarero:	Hay anchoas, aceitunas, calamares fritos, chorizo …
Carmen:	**Una ración de calamares** y una de aceitunas, por favor.
Camarero:	En seguida, señores.

Ordering drinks

¿Qué van a tomar, señores?	What will you have?
¿Quieren algo para comer?	Do you want anything to eat?
Hay anchoas, aceitunas, chorizo … calamares fritos	We have anchovies, olives, garlic sausage, fried squid
En seguida…	At once
¿Qué tomas?	What'll you have?
Una coca-cola, por favor	A coke, please
Para mí un vermut	For me a vermouth
… con hielo y limón	… with ice and lemon
Quiero un zumo de naranja	I want an orange-juice
Yo quiero un vaso de vino tinto	I'd like a glass of red wine
Una cerveza, por favor	A beer, please
¿Qué tapas hay?	What small dishes do you have?

Las bebidas (drinks)

el vino tinto/ blanco/rosado	red/white/rosé wine
seco/dulce	dry/sweet
el jerez fino/amon- tillado/oloroso	dry/medium dry/ sweet sherry
la cerveza	lager, beer
… de barril	draught beer
la sangría	wine punch
la ginebra	gin
el vermut	vermouth
la cubalibre	rum and coke

Los refrescos (soft drinks)

el café, café sólo	black coffee
café con leche	white coffee
la leche	milk
el agua	water
el té	tea
té con leche	tea with milk
el chocolate	chocolate
un batido	milkshake
una naranjada	orangeade
una limonada	lemonade
una gaseosa	white lemonade

1 BAR AND SOCIAL

How to ask

Un tinto, por favor	A red wine, please	Un vaso de ...	A glass of ...
Una botella de ...	A bottle of ...	Un zumo de ...	A ... juice
Que esté bien frío	Nice and cold	... naranja/limón	... orange/lemon
Con hielo	With ice	Una taza de ...	A cup of ...
con gas/sin gas	fizzy/still	una coca-cola	coke

Las tapas (appetizers)

(Use 'una ración de' when asking for a portion.)

salchichón	salami sausage	jamón serrano	cured ham
queso	cheese	gambas	prawns
champiñones	mushrooms	mejillones	mussels
aceitunas	olives	anchoas	anchovies
cacahuetes	peanuts	almejas	clams
patatas fritas	crisps	calamares	squid
tortilla española	Spanish omelette	pulpo	octopus
chorizo	spiced and seasoned pork sausage	sepia	cuttlefish

Snacks

Although **tapas** can be very substantial, if you want something even more filling you can buy many different kinds of takeaway food. Street-vendors sell **helados** (ice-creams) and **churros** (long, thin sticks of fried batter dipped in sugar).

Los bocadillos (sandwiches made with French-type bread)

un bocadillo de queso/de jamón	a cheese/ham sandwich
de calamar/de tortilla	a squid/omelette sandwich
¿Qué bocadillos hay?	What sandwiches are there?
Uno de queso, por favor	A cheese one please

Other snacks

un sandwich (caliente)	toasted sandwich	¿Es para tomar ahora?	Is it to eat now?
una hamburguesa	hamburger	Para llevar	To take away
un helado de vainilla/de fresa	a vanilla/strawberry ice-cream		
de chocolate/de pistacho	a chocolate/pistachio ice-cream		

1 BAR AND SOCIAL

the way it works

People and things

The word for 'a' is **un** for masculine words and **una** for feminine words: e.g.: **un** vas**o** (a glass), **una** cas**a** (a house)

In the plural **un** becomes **unos** and **una** becomes **unas**: e.g. uno**s** calamar**es** (some squid), una**s** aceituna**s** (some olives)

There is, there are

Note the following expression from the dialogue:
Hay una vista maravillosa   There is a wonderful view
Hay is used in both singular and plural, and is the same in question form:
¿Qué tapas **hay**?   What tapas are there?
Hay anchoas   There are anchovies

Describing people and places

Adjectives such as modern**o** (= modern), maravillos**a** (= wonderful), bonit**o** (= pretty) have -**o** and -**a** endings which change according to the gender of the word they accompany, e.g.

una cocina modern**a**; una vista maravillos**a** (feminine)
un cuarto bonit**o**; **un** cuarto modern**o** (masculine)
una casa viej**a** (an old house)
un jardín pequeñ**o** (a small garden)

Some adjectives, however, including grand**e** (= big), and amabl**e** (= kind), do not change in the singular. *Note*: adjectives usually follow the noun.

With a plural word most adjectives add an -**s**: e.g. uno**s** cuarto**s** bonito**s**.

Going places

¿Cuándo **vamos**?   When do we go?
Vamos el miércoles   We are going on Wednesday

Vamos is part of the verb **ir** (to go). Here is the present tense:

voy	I go, am going	**vamos**	we go, are going
vas	you go, are going	**vais**	you go, are going
va	he/she/it goes, is going you go (formal)	**van**	they go, are going you go (formal)

Saying what you want

One of the first things you need to say is 'I want'. You can do this simply by stating the object and adding 'please', e.g. **Una coca-cola, por favor**. Or say:

Quiero una coca-cola (from **querer**, to want)	I want a coca-cola
Queremos unas tapas	We want some tapas

1 BAR AND SOCIAL

The complete pattern of the present tense of **querer** is as follows:

quiero	I want	queremos	we want
quieres	you want	queréis	you want
quiere	he/she wants	quieren	they want
	you want (formal)		you want (formal)

things to do

1.4 **¿Cómo es tu casa?** Can you describe your own house or flat? Use some of the words on page 10 e.g. moderno/viejo/bonito/grande/pequeño.

1 ¿La casa? Es grande.   4 ¿El cuarto de baño?
2 ¿El cuarto de estar?   5 ¿El jardín?
3 ¿La cocina?   6 ¿Tu cuarto de dormir?

1.5 You are in a café with a group of people. The waiter asks you what you want: **¿Qué quieren ustedes?**
You are the only person who can talk Spanish so you do the talking . . .

Ann: [a white coffee]   Un café con leche, por favor.
Thomas: [a red wine]
Alice: [a coke]
Isabel: [a cup of tea with lemon]
Martin: [a beer]

Now choose what you want yourself: Y yo quiero . . .

1.6 It is time for a snack. First you go to a café-bar to buy a sandwich:
Camarero: ¿Qué va a tomar, señor/a?
You: [Ask what sandwiches there are]
Camarero: Hay jamón, queso, chorizo, calamar . . .
You: [Say you'd like a ham sandwich please]
Camarero: En seguida, señor/a.

Next you spot an ice-cream stand . . .

You: [Ask what ice-creams there are]
Ice-cream seller: Tengo vainilla, fresa, chocolate, limón, pistacho . . .
You: [Say you want a strawberry one please]

1.7 Can you sort out which question goes with which answer?
1 ¿Qué tomas?   **(a)** Está en el garaje.
2 ¿Cómo se llama la madre?   **(b)** El domingo.
3 ¿Cómo es la casa?   **(c)** Una cerveza, por favor.
4 ¿Dónde está el coche?   **(d)** Es muy moderna.
5 ¿Cuándo vamos a la playa?   **(e)** Se llama Caterina.

11

2 GIVING PERSONAL DETAILS

TALKING ABOUT YOURSELF

¿de dónde es?/where are you from?

While Carmen is at work Tom is arranging to hire a car for Thursday and the manager is filling in a form and asking him some questions.

Gerente: Usted no es español, ¿verdad?

Tom: **No, no soy español, soy inglés.**

Gerente: Habla muy bien el español, señor.

Tom: Muchas gracias. **Mi esposa es española. Es de Santander.**

Gerente: ¿Es usted de Londres?

Tom: No, no soy de Londres. **Vivo en Southampton** pero **trabajo en Londres.**

Gerente: ¿En qué trabaja?

Tom: **Soy director de una empresa de computadoras.**

Gerente: ¿Está aquí de negocios?

Tom: No, yo estoy de vacaciones pero mi esposa está de negocios. **Es periodista.**

Gerente: ¿Y su dirección aquí en Madrid, por favor?

Tom: Es la calle del Duque de Sesto 72, tercer piso.

Gerente: Muy bien. **Tiene su permiso de conducir, ¿verdad?**

Tom: Sí. **Aquí tiene usted.**

2 GIVING PERSONAL DETAILS

Nationality and language

¿Es usted español?	Are you Spanish?
No, soy inglés/inglesa	No, I'm English
Soy alemán/americano	I'm German/American
Son galesas/escocesas	They are Welsh/Scottish
Mi esposa es española	My wife is Spanish
Mi marido es español	My husband is Spanish
Hablo el inglés	I speak English
¿Habla usted el francés?	Do you speak French?
No hablo el español	I don't speak Spanish
Hablo un poco de alemán	I speak a little German
Entiendo/No entiendo ...	I understand/I don't understand ...
Habla muy bien el español	You speak Spanish very well
Hable más despacio, por favor	Speak more slowly please

Where are you from?

¿Es usted de Londres?	Are you from London?
Es de Santander	She is from Santander
Soy de Edinburgo	I am from Edinburgh
¿De dónde eres?	Where are you from?
¿Dónde vive usted? Vivo en ...	Where do you live? I live in ...
Su dirección, por favor	Your address, please

What do you do? (see also list on p. 80)

¿En qué trabaja usted?	What is your job?
¿En qué trabajas?	What do you do for a living?
Soy director	I am a director
una empresa de computadoras	a computer firm
trabajo en ...	I work in ...
¿Está aquí de negocios?	Are you here on business?
Estoy de vacaciones	I am on holiday
Es periodista	She is a journalist

Note: to say 'I am a teacher', etc. in Spanish you say: **Soy profesor**, etc., i.e. without using the indefinite article.

Documents

Su pasaporte, por favor	Your passport, please
¿Tiene su permiso de conducir?	Do you have your driving licence?
Aquí tiene usted	Here you are

How old are you?

¿Cuántos años tiene/tienes?	How old is he/are you?
Tiene dos años	He is two
Tengo cuarenta y cinco años	I'm 45

Marital status

Soy casado/casada	I am married	**Soy soltero/soltera**	I am single

2 GIVING PERSONAL DETAILS

the way it works

Talking about yourself

When talking about yourself, your nationality, where you are from, what your profession is, etc., you always use the verb **ser**.

Soy inglés	I am English
Somos de Manchester	We are from Manchester
Es estudiante	He is a student

Verb groups

Note these expressions from the dialogues:

Habla muy bien el español	You speak Spanish very well
Trabajo en Londres	I work in London

These examples come from a group of regular Spanish verbs, the **-ar** group, so called because all the infinitives (or dictionary forms) end in **-ar**. The present tense of these verbs is as follows:

hablar, *to speak*

habl-**o**	I speak	habl-**amos**	we speak
habl-**as**	you speak	habl-**áis**	you speak
habl-**a**	he/she speaks	habl-**an**	they speak
habl-**a**	you speak (formal)	habl-**an**	you speak (formal)

There are two other verb groups, the **-er** group and the **-ir** group. Here is a regular example of the **-er** group:

beber, *to drink*

beb-**o**	I drink	beb-**emos**	we drink
beb-**es**	you drink	beb-**éis**	you drink
beb-**e**	he/she drinks/	beb-**en**	they drink/
	you drink (formal)		you drink (formal)

and one of the **-ir** group:

vivir, *to live*

viv-**o**	I live	viv-**imos**	we live
viv-**es**	you live	viv-**ís**	you live
viv-**e**	he/she lives/	viv-**en**	they live/
	you live (formal)		you live (formal)

Do you have ...? (¿Tiene ...?)

¿Tiene su permiso de conducir?	Do you have your driving licence?
Aquí **tiene** usted.	Here you are (literally 'you have it')

These phrases contain examples of the verb **tener** (to have), which is used very frequently. It conveys the idea of *possession* and *availability*. It is also used when talking about *age*:

¿Cuántos años **tienes**?	How old are you? (literally, 'how many years do you have?')
Tengo 23 años	I'm 23

We will also meet **tener** + **que**, when it means 'to have to':

Tengo que ir al dentista	I have to go to the dentist.

2 GIVING PERSONAL DETAILS

Here is the complete pattern of the present tense:

tengo	I have	**tenemos**	we have
tienes	you have	**tenéis**	you have
tiene	he/she/it has	**tienen**	they have
tiene	you have (formal)	**tienen**	you have (formal)

things to do

2.1 **¿En qué trabajas?** (What do you do?) Can you sort out what everyone does by linking them with their place of work?

1	Soy	secretaria	Trabajo en	**(a)**	un hospital
2		profesor		**(b)**	una fábrica (factory)
3		enfermera		**(c)**	una tienda (shop)
4		mecánico		**(d)**	una oficina
5		ingeniero		**(e)**	un garaje
6		dependienta		**(f)**	un colegio

2.2 You do it too! (Use también = too, also)
Example: Carmen habla el español. Yo también hablo el español.

1 Luisa habla el inglés.
2 Juan estudia idiomas
   (studies languages)
3 Tom trabaja en Londres.
4 Carmen y Tom hablan español.
   Nosotros también ...
5 Miguel y Luisa estudian el español.
   Nosotros también ...

2.3 Can you describe your friend? Here are some useful words: amable (kind), alto (tall), grande (big), bajo (short), simpático (nice), gordo (fat), guapa (pretty)

You are asked to describe your Spanish friends to someone who wants to meet them. Here is the description of Miguel.

"Se llama Miguel. Miguel es inglés. Es de Londres. Habla el español y el inglés. Tiene 14 años. Es alto y delgado (= slim). Tiene una hermana que se llama Luisa."

1 Eduardo (from Madrid – accountant aged 24 – short and fat – one brother)
2 Can you describe yourself? *(See p.80 for list of jobs)*
   Me llamo ... (your name)   Soy de ... (where you are from)
   Vivo en ... (where you live)   Soy ... (what you do)
   Trabajo en ... (where you work)   Tengo ... (your age)

2.4 Everyone is telling you where they live.

1 Yo ... en Madrid. ¿Dónde ... usted?
2 Yo ... en Tarragona, pero mi hermano ... en Valencia.
3 Nosotros ... en Toledo. Y vosotros, ¿dónde ...?
4 Y ellos, dónde ...? ¿En Salamanca? No, ... en Ciudad Real.

TRAVEL ENQUIRIES/TIME

¿qué hora es?/what's the time?

Juan and Luisa are having lunch together. Juan has a sudden thought . . .

Juan: **¿Qué hora es, por favor?**
Luisa: Pues, **son las tres y media** . . .
Juan: ¡Hombre! ¿Son ya las tres y media? ¡Me voy ahora mismo! Tengo una cita con el dentista a las cuatro y cuarto. **Adiós, hasta luego.**
Luisa: **Hasta luego.**

Telling the time

¿Qué hora es, por favor?	What is the time, please?
¿Son ya las tres y media?	Three-thirty already?
Me voy ahora mismo	I must go this very minute
Tengo una cita con el dentista	I have a dentist appointment
a las cuatro y cuarto	at a quarter past four
antes/después	before/after

Saying goodbye

Adiós	Goodbye	**Hasta la vista**	Till we meet again
Hasta luego	See you later	**Hasta el sábado**	Till Saturday

2 USING PUBLIC TRANSPORT

Spanish trains   The Spanish National Rail Network is called **RENFE** (Red Nacional de los Ferrocarriles Españoles). There are many different sorts of train, and variations in fares, so it is necessary to be specific when asking for information. Here is a list of the main trains.

el tranvía/ómnibus	slow, stopping strain
el rápido	fast but stopping train
el expreso	long-distance night train, slowish
el TALGO/TER/TAFF	inter-city express
el AVE	inter-city express between Madrid and Sevilla.

You pay a supplement to travel on many fast or long-distance trains. The cheapest days to travel are Blue Days (**Díaz Azules**) when for long journeys you can normally get a 20% reduction on individual return tickets. Other discounts are available for families, parties, senior citizens, etc. Tickets bought in advance include a seat reservation. Advance booking is recommended, especially for inter-city trains.

¿ a qué hora hay tren?/when is there a train?

When Juan returns he telephones the RENFE office (**la oficina de viajes RENFE**) to find out the times of the trains to Santander the next day.

Empleada:	Dígame.
Juan:	Buenos días. **¿A qué hora hay trenes para Santander**, por favor?
Empleada:	¿Cúando quiere viajar?
Juan:	**Mañana por la mañana.**
Empleada:	**El Talgo sale a las ocho veinticinco** y hay un rápido a las once treinta.
Juan:	**¿A qué hora llega el Talgo a Santander?**
Empleada:	A las catorce cuarenta y cinco.
Juan:	**¿Hay que reservar asientos en el Talgo?**
Empleada:	Sí, señor.
Juan:	Gracias, señorita.
Empleada:	De nada. Adiós.

2 USING PUBLIC TRANSPORT

BUYING A TICKET
en el despacho de billetes/in the ticket office

The three go to Chamartín station to buy the tickets for the next day.

Empleada:	¿Qué desean ustedes?
Juan:	**Tres billetes de segunda clase para Santander**, por favor.
Empleada:	Sí, señor. ¿De ida o de ida y vuelta?
Juan:	**De ida y vuelta.**
Empleada:	¿Para qué tren?
Juan:	**Para mañana, para el Talgo** de las ocho veinticinco.
Empleada:	Muy bien. Aquí tienen sus billetes.
Juan:	Gracias. **¿Cuánto es, por favor?**
Empleada:	Son veinticinco mil pesetas.
Juan:	Hay restaurante en el tren, ¿verdad?
Empleada:	Sí, señor.

Station notices

Estación de ferrocarril	Railway station
Trenes de cercanías	Local/suburban trains
Trenes de largo recorrido	Long-distance trains
Despacho de billetes	Ticket-office
Llegadas/Salidas	Arrivals/Departures
Sala de espera/Consigna	Waiting-room/Left-luggage
Horario/Destino	Timetable/Destination

Train enquiries

la agencia de viajes	travel agency
la taquilla	ticket window
Venta anticipada	Sale of tickets in advance
¿A qué hora hay trenes para ...?	At what time are there trains for ...?
¿A qué hora sale ...?	What time does it leave?
¿A qué hora es el próximo tren para ...?	What time is the next train to ...?
¿Cuándo quiere viajar?	When do you want to travel?
Mañana por la mañana/por la tarde	Tomorrow morning/afternoon
El Talgo sale ...	The Talgo leaves at ...
¿A qué hora llega ...?	What time does it arrive?
¿Hay que reservar asientos?	Does one have to book seats?
¿Hay que pagar suplemento?	Does one have to pay a supplement?
¿Hay restaurante/coche-cama?	Is there a restaurant-car/sleeping-car?
¿Hay coche-literas?	Are there couchettes?
¿De qué andén sale?	Which platform does it leave from?
Vía número tres	Platform three
¿Lleva retraso?	Is it late?
¿Cuánto tiempo tarda?	How long does it take?
fumador/no fumador	smoker/non-smoker

2 USING PUBLIC TRANSPORT

Travelling by bus and coach   City buses are usually pay-as-you-enter and are run on a flat fare system. Before getting on the bus check which number and route you want on the bus-stop sign. In Madrid, as well as the normal buses of the state-run EMT (Empresa Municipal de Transportes), there are also privately-run minibuses which are more expensive.

Coaches link Madrid with the provincial capitals and some villages and towns. Coach fares are fixed by the length of the journey, and on some long-distance routes tickets are obtainable in advance.

Bus enquiries (see also train section above)

¿A qué hora hay autobús/autocar para . . .?	What time is there a bus/coach to . . .?
es el próximo autobús?	the next bus?
es el último autobús?	the last bus?
Hay uno a . . .	There's one at . . .
¿De dónde sale?	Where does it leave from?
Parada/Estación de autobuses	bus stop/station
plazas libres	seats free
completo	bus full
Entrega de equipajes	Baggage in
Recogida de equipajes	Baggage collection

Buying a ticket

un billete	a ticket
Tres billetes para Santander	Three tickets to Santander
de segunda clase/de primera clase	second/first class
de ida/de ida y vuelta	single/return
¿Para qué tren?	For which train?
No quedan billetes	There are no tickets left
Aquí tienen sus billetes	Here are your tickets
¿Cuánto es?	How much is it?
una reserva de asiento	seat reservation
¿Hay reducciones para niños?	Are there reductions for children?
Sólo para menores de 12 años	Only for children under 12
¿Hay reducciones para estudiantes?	Are there student reductions?
una tarjeta familiar	a family ticket
un billete entero	one full-price ticket
un billete de niño	one child's ticket

2 USING PUBLIC TRANSPORT

Plan of the Madrid Underground (Metro)

▬▬▬ Line 1
▬▬▬ Line 2
▬▬▬ Line 3
▬▬▬ Line 4
▬▬▬ Line 5
▬▬▬ Line 6
▬▬▬ Line 7
▬▬▬ Ramal
▬▬▬ Suburbano
▬ ▬ ▬ under construction

Listen for the following phrases

Vía número cuatro	Platform/Track four
El tren con destino a …	The train for …
El tren procedente de …	The train from …

►►► **Travelling by metro**   There are good underground metro systems in Madrid and Barcelona, open from 5 am to 11 pm. Fares are inexpensive and are organised on a flat-fare basis. When you buy a ticket check which line you want (**Línea**) and the name of the last station on the line (**Dirección**). To make a connection look for the sign which says **Correspondencias**.

Metro travel

Uno, por favor	One ticket, please
¿Qué línea es para …?	What line is it for …?
La dos	Number two
¿Tengo que hacer transbordo?	Do I have to change?
No, es directo	No, it's direct
Sí, en Goya	Yes, at Goya station
Línea/Dirección	Line/direction
Correspondencia	connection
Devuelve cambio	Change given
Precio exacto	Exact money

SALIDA

BILLETES

2 USING PUBLIC TRANSPORT

Air travel enquiries

¿A qué hora hay vuelos a Sevilla?	At what time are there flights to Seville?
¿Hay un vuelo a Londres hoy?	Is there a flight to London today?
Hay uno a las once de la mañana	There's one at eleven in the morning
Quisiera reservar un asiento	I'd like to book a seat
¿Es un vuelo directo?	Is it a direct flight?
¿Dónde está el terminal aéreo?	Where is the air terminal?

Taxis   Fares vary in different areas but taxi-drivers should have a list of approved fares for inner-city runs. There is a basic initial charge, and additional surcharges will be added to the meter at night, weekends and holidays.

Other notices

Parada de autobuses	Bus stop
Estación de autobuses	Coach station
Parada de taxis	Taxi stand
Oficina de Información	Information Office
Vuelos internacionales	International flights
Vuelos nacionales	Domestic flights
Salida	Exit

Asking and telling the time/¿Qué hora es?

To ask the time in Spanish use the verb **ser**: **¿Qué hora es?** What is the time?

The answer is either **Es la una** (It's one o'clock) or: **Son las dos, tres, etc** (it's two, three o'clock). (For numbers, see p.79).

Son las dos y cinco	It's 2.05	Son las tres menos cinco	It's 2.55
Son las dos y diez	It's 2.10	Son las tres menos diez	It's 2.50
Son las dos y cuarto	It's 2.15	Son las tres menos cuarto	It's 2.45
Son las dos y veinte	It's 2.20	Son las tres menos veinte	It's 2.40
Son las dos y veinticinco	It's 2.25	Son las tres menos veinticinco	It's 2.35
Son las dos y media	It's 2.30		

To say 'am' and 'pm' you say:

Son las diez **de la mañana**	It's 10.00 am	A las cinco **de la tarde**	At 5 pm
Son las diez **de la noche**	It's 10.00 pm		

24-hour clock

Official time in Spain is calculated on the 24-hour clock. So for train, bus and air timetables, opening and closing times, etc. be prepared to hear, for example, the following:

2 USING PUBLIC TRANSPORT

El vuelo número IB367 con destino a Londres sale a las quince veinte.

El expreso sale de Madrid a las dieciocho veinte y llega a Murcia a las seis de la mañana.

Note that the 24-hour clock leaves out **y** and **menos**: quince veinte = 15.20; quince cincuenta = 15.50

How to say to and from, etc.

De is used to mean 'of' or 'from':

Sale **de** Madrid	It leaves *from* Madrid
las ocho **de** la mañana	8 o'clock *in* the morning
de segunda clase	second class
la maleta **de** Luisa	Luisa's suitcase (suitcase *of* Luisa)

A means 'at or 'to':

¿**A** qué hora?	*At* what time?
Voy **a** Santander	I'm going *to* Santander
Llega **a** Santander	It arrives *at* Santander
a las diecinueve cuarenta	*at* 19.40

Another useful word in this dialogue is **para**, which means 'for'.

los trenes **para** Santander	the trains *for* Santander (para = destination)
para dos personas	*for* two people
para hoy/**para** mañana	*for* today/for tomorrow BUT
por la mañana	*in* the morning (por = *during*)

It leaves at ten

Sale a los ocho veinticinco	It leaves at 8.25. (from **salir**)
Llega a las catorce	It arrives at 14.00 (from **llegar**)

You will find both these verbs are very useful. While **llegar** is a regular **-ar** verb (like **trabajar**), **salir** is an **-ir** verb with an irregular first person form:

salgo	I leave	**salimos**	we leave
sales	you leave	**salís**	you leave
sale	he/she/it leaves/ you leave (formal)	**salen**	they leave/ you leave (formal)

things to do

2.5 **¿Qué hora es?** You are with a group of people and someone stops you to ask the time. The trouble is that everyone's watch says something different! **Son las . . .**

22

2 USING PUBLIC TRANSPORT

2.6 ¿A qué hora hay autobús para Segovia?

Destino	Salida	Destino	Salida
Segovia	10.15	Badajoz	5.45
Ávila	15.30	Huelva	9.30
Valladolid	10.35	Toledo	11.25

Can you say what time the buses run, e.g.:
¿A qué hora hay autobús para Segovia?   Hay uno a las diez y cuarto.

1 ¿A qué hora hay autobús para Toledo?
2 ¿A qué hora hay autobús para Ávila?
3 ¿A qué hora hay autobús para Badajoz?
4 ¿A qué hora hay autobús para Huelva?
5 ¿A qué hora hay autobús para Valladolid?

2.7 Look at the price information sheet and answer:

	Ida	Ida y vuelta
Madrid – Santander	5.000 ptas	8.500 ptas
Madrid – Barcelona	5.500 ptas	9.500 ptas
Madrid – Torremolinos	6.000 ptas	10.000 ptas

1 Quiero un billete de ida para Santander. ¿Cuánto es? Son . . .
2 Quiero un billete de ida y vuelta para Barcelona. ¿Cuánto es? Son . . .
3 Quiero un billete de ida para Torremolinos. ¿Cuánto es? Son . . .

2.8 1 You overhear the booking-clerk advising a passenger about trains.
Can you guess what the passenger is asking?

Passenger: ¿...?
Clerk: El próximo tren para Sevilla sale a las nueve doce.
Passenger: ¿...?
Clerk: Llega a las quince treinta.

2 **En el metro.** Juan wants to go to Colón station for his dentist
appointment. Can you fill in his part of the conversation?

Juan: [One, please]
Clerk: Aquí tiene. Ciento ochenta pesetas.
Juan: [Ask what line for Colón]
Clerk: Es la cuatro.
Juan: [Ask if you have to change]
Clerk: No, es directo.

3 SHOPPING AND MONEY

BUYING CLOTHES, SOUVENIRS

Shopping   Shops are usually open from 9.30 am to 1.30 pm and from 4 pm to 7.30 or 8.00 pm. As in Britain, department stores sell a wide range of goods, including furniture (**muebles**), records (**discos**), clothes (**ropa**), gifts (**regalos**), etc. Most credit cards (**tarjetas de crédito**) are accepted. Prices do not always include **IVA** (Spanish VAT) which may be added on as an extra.

los grandes almacenes/the department store

Carmen wants to buy a leather jacket and she sets off for the Nuevas Galerías (a big department store). There she talks to the shop assistant.

Dependienta:	¿Qué desea, señora?
Carmen:	**Quisiera una chaqueta du cuero.**
Dependienta:	¿Es para usted? ¿Cuál es su talla?
Carmen:	**La cuarenta y dos**.
Dependienta:	(shows her some) ¿Le gusta este estilo?
	Tenemos en negro, marrón y azul oscuro.
Carmen:	Sí, **el estilo me gusta, pero no me gusta el color.**
	Me gusta más la negra - es más elegante.
	¿Puedo probármela, por favor?
Dependienta:	Sí, señora. Pase por aquí, por favor.

(Carmen tries it on but finds it too small.)

3 SHOPPING AND MONEY

Carmen: ¡Qué lástima! No me sienta bien. **Es demasiado pequeña.** ¿Me puede enseñar otra más grande?

Dependienta: Claro, señora, aquí está. (she tries it on) ¿Qué le parece?

Carmen: Sí, me parece muy bien. **¿Cuánto cuesta, por favor?**

Dependienta: Cuesta viente mil quinientas pesetas.

Carmen: Bueno, **la compro**.

Shopping – sizes and colours

¿Qué desea, señora?	What do you want?
¿Es para usted?	Is it for you?
¿Cuál es su talla?	What is your size?
¿Qué número tiene?	What size do you take? (shoes)
¿Le gusta este estilo/color?	Do you like this style/colour?
Tenemos en negro/en marrón/en azul	We have it in black/brown/blue
Los probadores están allí	The changing rooms are over there
Pase por aquí, por favor	Come this way, please
¿Algo más?	Do you want anything else?
Lo siento	I'm sorry
Es lo/la más barato/a que tenemos	It is the cheapest we have
Sólo quiero mirar	I'm just looking
Quiero/Quisiera	I want/I'd like ...
una chaqueta de cuero	a leather jacket
(Mi talla) es la cuarenta y dos	My size is a 42 ...
Mi número es ...	My size is ... (shoes)
Me gusta/no me gusta	I like it/I don't like it
el color/el estilo	the colour/the style
¿Tiene algo en rojo/verde?	Do you have anything in red/green?
Me gusta más ...	I prefer ...
Es más elegante	It's more elegant
Me gusta mucho	I like it very much
¿Puedo probármelo/probármela?	Can I try it on?
Me sienta bien (no me sienta)	It fits me (doesn't fit me)
Es demasiado pequeño/a, grande, corto/a, largo/a, caro/a	It's too small, big, short, long, expensive
¿Hay otro más grande?/más barato?	Is there a bigger one?/cheaper one?
¿Me puede enseñar otro/a ...?	Can you show me another ...?
¿Cuánto cuesta?	How much is it?
Me lo quedo/me la quedo	I'll have it
Lo/la compro	I'll take it

USEFUL WORDS AND PHRASES

¿Qué le parece?	What do you think?
Me parece muy bien	I think it's fine
¡Qué lástima!	What a pity!
OFERTA/REBAJAS	SALE BARGAINS

	Clothes sizes – women						
British	8	10	12	14	16	18	20
Spanish	36	38	40	42	44	46	48

	Collar sizes – men							
British	13	13½	14	14½	15	15½	16	16½
Spanish	34	35	36	37	38	39	40	41

	Shoe sizes									
British	2	3	4	5	6	7	8	9	10	11
Spanish	35	36	37	38	39	40	41	42	43	44

¿algo más?/anything else?

In Spain you do not normally need to go to the post-office to buy stamps – you can buy them in an **estanco** which usually sells postcards and stamps as well as tobacco and cigarettes (**cigarrillos**), and sometimes newspapers as well. Tom is choosing some postcards, but he is unlucky with the stamps . . .

Tom:	**Quiero estas cuatro postales, por favor.**
Dependente	Sí, señor. Las postales cuestan quince pesetas.
Tom:	Y **¿tiene usted sellos?** Quiero cuatro para Inglaterra.
Dependiente:	No señor. **Tiene que ir a Correos. ¿Algo más?**
Tom:	¿Tiene periódicos ingleses?
Dependiente:	Me parece que tengo uno … Pero no lo veo. Lo siento, señor, no queda ninguno. Hay un quiosco en la esquina.
Tom:	Gracias, entonces, **eso es todo**.

Buying holiday items

Quiero estas cuatro postales	I want these four postcards
¿Tiene usted sellos?	Do you have stamps?
Cuatro para Inglaterra	Four stamps for England
Tiene que ir a Correos	You'll have to go to the post-office
¿Tiene usted periódicos/revistas ingleses?	Do you have English papers/ magazines?
Me parece que tengo uno	I think I have one
Pero no lo veo. No queda ninguno	But I don't see it. There are none left.
Eso es todo	That's all

3 SHOPPING AND MONEY

Quiero un mapa	I want a map
… una pila, un carrete	… a battery, a film
… un porrón, un collar	… a wine-jar, a necklace

the way it works

This and that

The word for 'this' is **este** for masculine nouns and **esta** for feminine nouns:

este estilo	this style;	**esta** chaqueta	this jacket

To say 'that' you normally use **ese, esa**:

ese color	that colour;	**esa** camisa	that shirt

In the plural the pattern is as follows:

est**os**, est**as**	these	es**os**, es**as**	those

To say 'this one' or 'that one' use **éste**, **ésta** or **ése**, **ésa** with an accent. In a less specific sense **esto, eso** can also mean 'this' and 'that'.

More or less

The word for 'more' is **más** and 'less' is **menos**: más grande (bigger); más pequeño (smaller); más caro (more expensive); más barato (cheaper).
To say 'bigger than' or 'more … than' you use **más … que**

Este traje es más grande que el otro. (bigger than the other)
Esta camisa es más cara que la otra. (more expensive than the other)

If you want to say 'biggest' or 'the most …' you can use **el/la más**:

Esta camisa es la más grande. (the biggest)
Este vestido es el más barato. (the cheapest)

Object pronouns

(1) Direct

¿El periódico? No **lo** veo	The newspaper? I don't see it
¿La chaqueta? **La** compro	The jacket? I'll have it
¿Los zapatos? Me **los** quedo	The shoes? I'll have them
¿Las postales? No **las** veo	The postcards? I don't see them

As well as *it* and *them* we sometimes use a person as the object, e.g. *me* or *you*:

La conozco/**las** conozco	I know her/them (fem.)
Le veo/**les** veo	I see him/them (masc.)
Me ve/**te** ve	He sees me/he sees you

Here is a list of direct object pronouns:

me	me	nos	us
te	you	os	you
le/la	him, her you (masc/fem)	les/las	them (people you (masc/fem)
lo/la	it (masc/fem)	los/las	them (things)

3 SHOPPING AND MONEY

(2) Indirect

¿**Me** puede enseñar otro?   Can you show *(to) me* another one?
¿Qué **le** parece?   What does it seem *to you*?

Here is a list of indirect object pronouns:

me	to me	nos	to us
te	to you	os	to you
le	to him/her	les	to them (people)
	to you		to you
le	to it	les	to them (things)

Note that the object pronoun normally comes *before* the verb. When the verb is in the infinitive, however, it may either precede or follow, in which case it is added on to the verb itself: ¿Puedo **probármela**? (Can I try it on?)

How to say 'I like it'

Look at the following phrases taken from the dialogues:

¿Le gusta este estilo?   Do you like this style?
Sí, me gusta   I like it
No me gusta el color   I don't like the colour
Me gusta más   I prefer
Me gusta mucho   I like it very much

From these examples you can see that the word 'like' is used in a different way to English. Me gusta el estilo (I like the style) really means 'the style is pleasing to me' (indirect object). With more than one thing use gust**an**.

Me gustan estas camisas   I like these shirts

Here is the verb in full:

me gusta(n)	I like	**nos gusta(n)**	we like
te gusta(n)	you like	**os gusta(n)**	you like
le gusta(n)	he/she likes	**les gusta(n)**	they like
le gusta(n)	you like (formal)	**les gusta(n)**	you like (formal)

things to do

3.1 Carmen is describing to her sister some of the clothes she has seen.
For colours and materials see p. 80.

1 Q. ¿El vestido (*dress*) es rojo y negro?
   A. Sí, es rojo y negro.
2 Q. ¿La falda (*skirt*) es verde?
3 Q. ¿La camisa (*shirt*) es amarilla?
   Y ¿es de seda o de algodón?
4 Q. ¿El suéter es marrón?
   Y ¿es de lana o de acrílico?
5 Q. ¿Los pantalones son grises?

3 SHOPPING AND MONEY

3.2 You are in a department store buying a tee-shirt (**una camiseta**). Can you fill in your part of the conversation?

Assistant: ¿Qué desea, señorita?
You: [Say you want a tee-shirt]
Assistant: ¿Qué talla tiene?
You: [Say you take a 40]
Assistant: ¿Le gusta ésta?
You: [Say you like the style but not the colour]
Assistant: La tenemos también en rojo y en azul.
You: [Say you prefer the blue. Ask if you can try it on]
Assistant: ¿Qué le parece, señorita?
You: [Say you like it and ask how much it is]
Assistant: Cuesta mil ochocientas cuarenta pesetas.
You: [Say you'll have it]

3.3 See how difficult it is to get a good fit!

Assistant: ¿Le gusta este traje?
You: No, es demasiado . . . ¿Hay otro más . . .?
Assistant: ¿Le gusta esta camisa?
You: ....
Assistant: ¿Le gusta este sombrero?
You: ....
Assistant: ¿Le gustan estos vaqueros?
You: Son .... Hay otros más . . .
Assistant: ¿Le gustan estos zapatos?
You: ....

3.4 ¿**Cuánto cuesta?** Can you say in Spanish the prices of these articles?

9.200   800   12.600   6.500   2.700

3.5 **Tienes que ir a la librería**. Can you match the following items with the shops where you can buy them? (see p. 81 for a list of shops)

1 una pila (battery)   **(a)** la ferretería
2 un diccionario (dictionary) **(b)** el quiosco
3 un perfume   **(c)** la tienda de aparatos eléctricos
4 un periódico (newspaper)   **(d)** la perfumería
5 un sacacorchos (corkscrew)   **(e)** la papelería
6 un mapa (map)   **(f)** la librería

3 SHOPPING AND MONEY

BUYING FOOD

▶ ▶ ▶ **Food shops**   There are several names for a grocer's shop in Spain –
tienda de comestibles, alimentación, tienda de ultramarinos. You can, of
course, also buy food in the market (**mercado**), and supermarket
(**supermercado**) and there are also increasing numbers of hypermarkets
(**hipermercados**).

en la tienda de comestibles/at the grocer's

Juan, Luisa and Miguel have arrived in Santander and are stocking up with
provisions.

Luisa:	A ver, ¿qué tenemos que comprar? Jamón, salchichas, chorizo, queso, mantequilla, leche, galletas, anchoas y fruta.
Dependiente:	Buenos días, señorita. ¿Qué desea?
Luisa:	**Deme doscientos gramos de jamón** . . ., **medio kilo de** salchichas . . ., **cien gramos de** chorizo . . ., medio kilo de este queso manchego . . ., cien gramos de mantequilla . . ., y **un litro de** leche, por favor.
Dependiente:	¿Algo más, señorita?
Luisa:	Sí. **Póngame un paquete de** esas galletas, y una lata de anchoas . . ., y **un kilo de** manzanas . . . Y ya está.
Miguel:	Oye, Luisa, mira estos melocotones. Me gustan muchísimo los melocotones y están bien maduros. ¿Qué te parece?

3 SHOPPING AND MONEY

Luisa:	Bueno, chico, **vamos a comprar medio kilo de melocotones para tí.** Y eso es todo. ¿Cuánto es, por favor?
Dependiente:	Son novecientas sesenta y cinco pesetas en total, señorita.
Luisa:	Vale. (hands him the money) ¿Tiene una bolsa de plástico, por favor?
Dependiente:	Aquí tiene. Adiós, señorita.

Shopping – food

¿Qué tenemos que comprar?	What do we have to buy?
Deme doscientos gramos de ...	Give me 200 grams of ...
este queso manchego	this manchegan cheese
... medio kilo de jamón	... half a kilo of ham
... cien gramos de mantequilla	... 100 grams of butter
... un litro de leche	... 1 litre of milk
¿Algo más?	Anything else?
Póngame un paquete de ...	Give me a packet of ...
esas galletas	those biscuits
... una lata de anchoas	... a tin of anchovies
... un kilo de manzanas	... a kilo of apples
una rodaja de ...	a slice of ...
un trozo de ...	a piece of ...
Y ya está	And that's it
Oye, Luisa, mira ...	Oh, Luisa, look at ...
estos melocotones	these peaches
Me gusta(n) muchísimo ...	I adore ...
Está(n) bien maduro(s)	It is/They are nice and ripe
¿Qué te parece?	What do you think?
Bueno, chico ...	Well ...
Vamos a comprar ...	We'll buy ...
¿Cuánto es, por favor?	How much is it?
Son novecientas sesenta y cinco ptas	That's 965 pesetas
Vale	O.K.
¿Tiene una bolsa de plástico?	Do you have a plastic bag?
Aquí tiene	Here you are
Congelados	frozen food
un poco más/menos	a little more/less
bastante/demasiado	enough/too much

CHANGING MONEY

Banking hours   9 am to 2 pm Monday to Friday, and 9 am to 1 pm on Saturday (but not in the summer). You can also change money in some shops and hotels, but you will get a better rate of exchange in a bank. Cash is also available from cashpoint machines (**cajeros automáticos**) with some credit cards. The unit of currency is the **peseta**. There 1,000, 2,000, 5,000 and 10,000 peseta notes (**billetes**) and 1, 5 (=**un duro**), 10, 25, 50, 100, 200 and 500 peseta coins (**monedas**).

3 SHOPPING AND MONEY

Tom goes to the bank to cash some traveller's cheques.

Tom:	Buenos días. **Quisiera cambiar unos cheques de viaje, por favor.**
Empleada:	Sí, señor. ¿Cuánto quiere cambiar?
Tom:	Cien libras. **¿A cómo está el cambio hoy?**
Empleada:	A ciento noventa y seis pesetas. ¿Su pasaporte, por favor? . . . Firme usted aquí. . . . Quiere pasar a la caja, por favor.
Cajero:	¿Cómo quiere su dinero, señor?
Tom:	Pues, **déme tres billetes de cinco mil pesetas** y el resto en billetes de menor valor.

Money language

Cambio	Exchange
Quisiera cambiar . . .	I'd like to change
unos cheques de viaje	some traveller's cheques
unas libras esterlinas	some pounds sterling
¿Cuánto quiere cambiar?	How much do you want to change?
Cien libras	£100
¿A cómo está el cambio?	What is the exchange rate . . .?
A ciento noventa y seis	196 pesetas
Firme usted aquí	Sign here
¿Quiere pasar a la caja?	Please go to the cash-desk
¿Cómo quiere su dinero?	How do you want your money?
Déme tres billetes	Give me three notes
el resto	the rest
menor valor	lesser value
¿Puede darme cambio?	Can you give me change?
las monedas	coins
los eurocheques	Eurocheques
la tarjeta de crédito	credit card
la carta de crédito	letter of credit
Quiero abrir una cuenta	I want to open an account
acreditar esto	to credit this

the way it works

Asking how much

There are several ways to ask the price of things. Here Luisa uses:

¿Cuánto es?   How much is it?

3 SHOPPING AND MONEY

You will also hear:

¿Cuánto cuesta/n?	How much is it/are they?
¿Cuánto vale/valen?	How much is it/are they (worth)?

In the bank Tom asks the exchange rate:

¿A cómo está el cambio?	What is the exchange rate?

We'll buy half a kilo/Vamos a comprar medio kilo.

The useful phrase **voy a ... + infinitive** is the simplest way of expressing the future tense:

Vamos a tomar una copa	We'll have a drink.
Voy a ver	I'll go and see
¿Qué **van a** tomar?	What will you have (to eat)?

things to do

.6 Your friend has a long shopping list. Can you tell him where to go for each item? (see also list on p. 81)

1	el pan	**(a)** la pastelería
2	la carne	**(b)** la tienda de comestibles
3	las naranjas	**(c)** la pescadería
4	la leche	**(d)** la frutería
5	el azúcar	**(e)** la panadería
6	el pescado	**(f)** la tienda de vinos
7	el vino	**(g)** la lechería
8	un pastel	**(h)** la carnicería

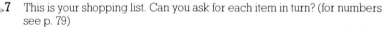

.7 This is your shopping list. Can you ask for each item in turn? (for numbers see p. 79)

250g butter
1 litre milk
500g ham
1 packet biscuits
1 tin sardines
1 kilo bananas
½ kilo peaches
6 pears
1 litre oil
2 bottles red wine
12 eggs

Start by saying: Quiero… Deme… Póngame…

3 SHOPPING AND MONEY

3.8 How much does it all cost? ¿Cuánto es todo?

Work out how much the following will cost you: un paquete de café; una docena de huevos; medio kilo de plátanos; dos kilos de tomates

3.9 You are in a tienda de comestibles buying various items.

Shopkeeper:	Hola, buenos días.
You:	[Say you want 200 grams of cheese and 100 grams of ham]
Shopkeeper:	¿Y algo más?
You:	[Ask for half a kilo of apples and 6 bananas]
Shopkeeper:	Muy bien. ¿Algo más?
You:	[Ask for a litre of milk. Say that's all and ask how much]

3.10 You are in a bank and you want to change some money.

You:	[Say good morning. You want to change some pounds]
Clerk:	¿Cuánto quiere cambiar?
You:	[£150. Ask what the exchange rate is]
Clerk:	A doscientas pesetas. Firme aquí, por favor, y pase a la caja.
Cashier:	¿Cómo quiere su dinero?
You:	[Say you want six 5,000 peseta notes.]

3.11 You are in a pastelería and your mouth is watering! (See list on p. 82)

Señora:	Puedo ayudarle?
You:	[Say you'd like two of those cakes and a tart]
Señora:	¿Algo más?
You:	[Say yes, ask her to give you a doughnut and bread-roll]
Señora:	¿Es para tomar ahora?
You:	[No it's to take away]

4 FINDING YOUR WAY

UNDERSTANDING DIRECTIONS

La Oficina de Turismo Most Spanish towns have a tourist office, which is usually the best place to obtain local maps and information about the region.

¿cómo puedo llegar a .../how do I get to ...?

Luisa and Miguel are trying to find their way around in Santander.

Luisa: ¿Dónde está la Oficina de Turismo por favor?

Passer-by: No está lejos. Van a pie, ¿verdad?

Luisa: Sí, vamos a pie.

Passer-by: Pues, **tomen la primera calle a la derecha y sigan todo derecho.** Al final de esa calle llegan ustedes a la Plaza. Está en la Plaza **a la izquierda** enfrente de la Catedral.

Luisa: Gracias, señor, ¿Y **hay un banco por aquí,** por favor?

Passer-by: Sí, señorita. Hay muchos bancos. **Cojan la segunda calle a la derecha.** Hay un banco en la esquina al lado de la biblioteca.

4 FINDING YOUR WAY

Miguel: ¿No **se puede coger un autobús?**

Luisa: ¡Qué perezoso eres! No, vamos andando. El banco está
             a unos diez minutos, nada más. Gracias, señora.

Passer-by: De nada, adiós.

Tom is driving to Ávila with Carmen. He is not
quite sure of the way out of Madrid.

Tom: **Perdón ¿la carretera de Ávila, por favor?**

Policeman: Pues, siga hasta el final de esta calle y doble a la derecha.
             Tome la segunda calle a la izquierda y allí está la carretera.
             Se llama la Avenida de la Princesa.

Tom: Gracias.

Asking the way

¿Dónde está la Oficina de Turismo?	Where is the tourist office?
No está lejos	It's not far away
¿Van a pie?	Are you on foot?
Si está cerca	If it's near
Tome(n) la primera calle	Take the first street
a la derecha/a la izquierda	on the right/on the left
siga(n) todo derecho	carry straight on
llegan ustedes	you'll arrive
a la Plaza	in the Square
enfrente de la Catedral	opposite the Cathedral
¿Hay un banco por aquí?	Is there a bank near here?
Hay muchos bancos	There are many banks
Coja la segunda calle	Take the second street
en la esquina	on the corner
al lado de la biblioteca	beside the library
¿No se puede coger un autobús?	Can't one take a bus?
Hay que coger un autobús	You must take a bus
Vamos andando/en coche/en autobús/	We'll go on foot/by car/by bus/
en taxi/en bicicleta/en motocicleta	by taxi/cycle/motorbike
Está a unos diez minutos	It's about ten minutes (walk)
¿La carretera de Ávila?	The road to Ávila?
Siga hasta el final de esta avenida	Go to the end of this avenue
Doble a la derecha	Turn right
¿Cómo puedo llegar a ...?	How can I get to ...?
la parada está allí enfrente	The bus stop is opposite
Cambie de autobús	Change buses

OTHER USEFUL PHRASES

¡Qué perezoso eres!	What a lazybones you are!
Perdón	Excuse me
¿Tiene un mapa de la ciudad?	Do you have a map of the city?

OFICINA DE TURISMO

4 FINDING YOUR WAY

the way it works

Asking for directions

There are several ways of asking for directions.

¿La Catedral, **por favor?**	The Cathedral, please?
¿**Dónde está** la estación?	*Where is the station?*
¿**Por dónde se va a** la playa?	*How does one get to the beach?*
¿**Cómo puede llegar al** albergue de juventud?	*How can I get to the youth hostel?*
¿**Para ir a** la playa?	*How does one get to the beach?*
¿**Hay** un banco **por aquí?**	*Is there a bank near here?*

Understanding instructions

Not only might you have to ask the way, but you will also have to be able to understand the various ways in which instructions are given in Spanish. Look at the following phrases:

Tomen la primera calle . . . **sigan** todo derecho . . . **Coja** la segunda calle . . . **Doble** a la derecha . . . **Tome** el número dos . . . **Cambie** de autobús

These forms of the verbs are known as the imperative (or command). The imperative is formed by taking the stem of the first person ('I' form) of the present tense (e.g. **tom**-o, **coj**-o, **sig**-o) and adding the following sets of endings:

For -**ar** verbs, e.g. **tomar** (to take) add -**e** (sing.), -**en** (pl.): **tome, tomen; doble, doblen**.

For -**er** and -**ir** verbs e.g. **seguir** (to follow), **subir** (to go up) add -**a** (sing.), -**an** (pl.): **siga, sigan; suba, suban**.

Note: the verb **ir** (to go) is irregular, the imperative being **vaya** (sing.) and **vayan** (pl.).

Methods of transport

Note the different ways of getting around: Vamos a pie, en tren, en coche, en avión, etc.

The verb **coger** is used for 'to catch' or 'take': 'To get on (a bus)' is **subir** and 'to get off' is **bajar**: **Subes** a la estación y **bajas** a la playa (You get on at the station and get off at the beach).

Place and distance words

The following expressions are essential for giving directions and it is worth listening out for them:

a la derecha	to/on the right	**al lado (de)**	beside
a la izquierda	to/on the left	**en la esquina**	on the corner
todo derecho	straight on	**al final (de)**	at the end (of
cerca (de)	near (to)	**allí**	there
lejos (de)	far (from)	**aquí**	here
aquí mismo	right here	**enfrente (de)**	opposite
hacia	towards	**hasta**	until, up to
por	along	**por aquí**	hereabouts
detrás (de)	behind	**delante (de)**	in front of
al otro lado	on the other side		

4   FINDING YOUR WAY

Notice the use of primero, segundo etc.

la primera calle a la derecha   the first street on the right
la segunda calle a la izquierda   the second street on the left

Also, you may be told how long it will take to get to your destination:

Está **a unos quince minutos.**   It's about fifteen minutes away.
Está **a una hora de viaje** de aquí.   It's an hour's journey from here.

and the distance:

Está **a doscientos metros**   It's 200 metres away
Está **a cien kilómetros**   It's 100 kilometres.

Poder (to be able) and volver (to return)

Some Spanish verbs change not only their endings but also the middle of the word.
In the case of both these -er verbs there is a vowel change from **o** to **ue** in the stem
of the 1st, 2nd and 3rd persons singular and 3rd plural.

pu**e**do	I can	podemos	we can
pu**e**des	you can (fam.)	podéis	you can (fam.)
pu**e**de	he/she/you can	pu**e**den	they/you can
vu**e**lvo	I return	volvemos	we return
vu**e**lves	you return (fam.)	volvéis	you return (fam.)
vu**e**lve	he/she returns, you return	vu**e**lven	they/you return

Impersonal se

To say 'Can one do this?' or 'How does one get to . . .?' Spanish uses an impersonal
pronoun **se** which is the equivalent of 'one', 'you', 'they' etc. before the third person
of the verb:

¿Por dónde **se va** a la playa?   How does one get to the beach?
¿**Se puede** aparcar aquí?   Can you park here?
¿Dónde **se puede** comprar el pan?   Where can one buy bread?
¿No **se puede** coger un taxi?   Can't we take a taxi?

The answer is formed in exactly the same way, namely:

Se va por la Plaza.   One goes through the Square.
Sí, **se puede.**/No, **no se puede.**   Yes, one can./No, one can't.

things to do

4.1   Can you work out how to get there? e.g.
¿Por donde se va a la catedral? ⟶ Tome la primera calle a la derecha.

1 ¿ . . . a la iglesia? (church) ⟵   3 ¿ . . . al parque? (park) ↑

2 ¿ . . . al museo? (museum) ⊐   4 ¿ . . . a la plaza? (square) ⌐

4 FINDING YOUR WAY

4.2 You are in the Calle de Castilla, by the station. (**X** marks the spot.) Look at the map and find out where you are being directed to:

1 Tome la primera calle a la izquierda y entonces la segunda a la derecha y siga todo derecho. Está a la izquierda.

2 Tome la tercera calle a la izquierda que se llama la Calle de la Lealtad y entonces la primera a la derecha. Está allí en la Plaza, enfrente de la Catedral.

3 Pase por delante de la Catedral hasta la Plaza Porticada. Está allí a la izquierda.

4 Tome la primera calle a la derecha y en seguida doble a la derecha otra vez. Está a la izquierda en la esquina.

5 Coja la primera calle a la izquierda y al final de esa calle tome la calle a la izquierda que se llama la Calle Alta. Siga todo recto hasta el final y está allí a la izquierda.

Key	(1) Aduana	(4) Plaza Porticada
	(2) Banco de España	(5) Oficina de Turismo
	(3) Catedral	(6) Ayuntamiento

4 FINDING YOUR WAY

MOTORING

Motoring   If you take your car to Spain, you must take with you your driving licence, car registration (log book) and adequate insurance. (The green card is still recommended.) It is advisable to take out a bail bond or extra insurance to cover legal costs in case of an accident. If you are stopped by the police for a traffic offence, you may be required to pay a fine on the spot. Speed limits are normally:

Motorways **(autopistas = A)**	120 km/h (75 mph)
National Highways **(carreteras nacionales = N)**	100 km/h (62 mph)
Other roads	90 km/h (56 mph)
Built-up areas	60 km/h (37 mph)

Motorways   There are currently about 2,500 km of motorway **(autopista)** in Spain, radiating out from Madrid. On most you pay a toll **(peaje)**, the amount depending on the distance covered.

4 FINDING YOUR WAY

en la gasolinera/at the petrol-station

Tom and Carmen are in the car driving to Ávila. They stop to buy petrol.

Empleada:	Buenas tardes, señor
Tom:	Buenas tardes. **Lleno, por favor**.
Empleada:	Bueno. Ya está, cuarenta y ocho litros.
Tom:	**¿Quiere comprobar el aceite y el agua**, por favor?
Empleada:	(Checks oil and water). Necesita medio litro de aceite.
Tom:	Muchas gracias. ¿Cuánto le debo?
Empleada:	Son cuatro mil trescientas pesetas.

el taller mecánico/the garage

Unfortunately, after setting off again, they have a puncture and after changing the wheel they call in at a garage on the outskirts of Ávila

Tom:	Hola, buenas tardes. Tengo un problema con el neumático. **¿Puede repararlo, por favor?**
Empleado:	Bueno, vamos a ver . . . Tiene un agujero bastante grande, pero creo que puedo hacerlo. ¿Puede volver dentro de un rato?
Tom:	Muy bien. Vuelvo en veinte minutos, ¿verdad?
Empleado:	Sí, señor.

Echando gasolina (putting in petrol)

Lleno, por favor	Fill it up, please
Dos mil pesetas por favor	2.000 pesetas of petrol
Cincuenta litros, por favor	50 litres
la gasolina	petrol
el gasóleo	diesel
la gasolina sin plomo	lead-free petrol
super/normal	= 4-star/= 2-star
¿Quiere comprobar . . . ?	Please could you check . . . ?
el aceite/el agua/la presión	oil/water/tyre pressure
Necesita medio litro	It needs half a litre
¿Cuánto le debo?	How much do I owe you?

Un pinchazo (a puncture)

el taller	garage, workshop
Arregla usted pinchazos?	Do you mend punctures?
¿Quiere reparar/arreglar . . . ?	Please repair/put right . . .
¿Puede cambiar . . . ?	Can you change . . . ?
el neumático	the tyre
Tiene un agujero	It has a hole
¿Puede volver dentro de un rato?	Please come back in a while

41

Mi coche está averiado (my car has broken down)

(parts of the car are listed on p. 82)

No funciona el motor	The engine is not working
Mi coche no quiere arrancar	My car won't start
¿Dónde está el garaje más cercano?	Where's the nearest garage?
¿Puede mandar un mecánico?	Can you send a mechanic?
¿Cuánto tiempo tardará?	How long will it take?
Puedo ponerlo en seguida	I can fit it at once
la marca/la matrícula	the make/the registration number

Road signs

Ceda el paso	Give way
¡Cuidado!	Caution
Desviación	Deviation
Dirección única	One-way street
Estacionamiento de automóviles	Car Park
Estacionamiento prohibido	No parking
Obras	Roadworks
Paso prohibido	No entry
Peatones	Pedestrians
Peligro	Danger
Puesto de socorro	First Aid

After an accident

Ha habido un accidente	There has been an accident
Hay gente herida	Some people are hurt
Llame la Policía	Call the police
Llame una ambulancia/un doctor	Call an ambulance/a doctor
¿Cuál es su nombre/su dirección?	What is your name/address?
su permiso de conducir	your driving licence
sus papeles de seguro	your insurance papers

OTHER USEFUL PHRASES

Ya está	That's it
Bueno, vamos a ver	Well, let's have a look
¿Cuánto le debo?	How much do I owe you?
Tengo un problema con ...	I have a problem with ...

ILLNESS AND INJURY

Illness   Since joining the EU in 1986, Spain has the same reciprocal health arrangements as the rest of the Union. Take with you your Form E111, obtainable from post offices in the UK. For minor ailments and injuries the local chemist (**farmacista**) is often helpful.

4 HEALTH AND EMERGENCY

me duele la cabeza/I have a headache

Pilar doesn't feel well and goes to the doctor.

Médico: Hola, buenas tardes, siéntese por favor.
Pilar: Buenas tardes, doctor.
Médico: Vamos a ver, ¿qué le pasa?
Pilar: **No me siento bien. Me duele la cabeza,** no tengo apetito y me parece que **tengo fiebre.**
Médico: ¿Desde cuándo se siente así, señora?
Pilar: Desde hace unos días . . . Y me siento mareada cuando me levanto por la mañana.
Médico: Por favor, tiéndase aquí. Voy a hacerle un examen. (Examines her) Por favor abra la boca . . . Respire profundo. . . . No se preocupe, señora, no es grave. Tiene gripe y debe quedarse en cama. Aquí tiene la receta . . . Tome dos cucharadas cada tres horas. ¡Adiós, que se mejore pronto!
Pilar: Gracias y adiós.

En el consultorio (in the doctor's surgery)

Siéntese por favor	Sit down please
¿Que le pasa?	What's wrong
No me siento bien	I don't feel well
Me duele la cabeza/ el estómago/los ojos	I have a headache/ a stomach-ache/eye-ache
No tengo apetito	I'm not hungry
Tengo fiebre	I have a temperature
Me siento mareada	I feel dizzy
cuando me levanto	when I get up
¿Desde cuándo se siente así?	How long have you been feeling like this?
Desde hace unos días	For a few days
Tiéndase aquí	Lie down
Voy a hacerle un examen	I'm going to examine you
Abra la boca	Open your mouth
Respire profundo	Breathe deeply
No se preocupe	Don't worry
No es grave	It's not serious
Tiene gripe	You have flu
Debe quedarse en cama	You must stay in bed
Aquí tiene la receta	Here is a prescription
Tome dos cucharadas	Take two spoonfuls
cada tres horas	every three hours
¡Qué se mejore pronte!	Get better soon!

4 HEALTH AND EMERGENCY

Things the doctor should know

Soy alérgico a ...	I'm allergic to ...
... la penicilina	... penicillin
Soy diabético	I'm diabetic
Tomo la píldora	I'm on the pill
Estoy embarazada	I'm pregnant

Things that can happen to you

(parts of the body are listed on p. 82)

Me duele el .../la ...	My ... hurts
Me he roto .../Me he quemado ...	I have broken .../I have burned ...
Me he torcido .../Me he cortado ...	I have twisted .../I have cut ...
Me ha picado un mosquito	A mosquito has stung me
Tengo una insolación	I have sunstroke
Tengo diarrea	I have diarrhoea
resfriado/catarro	a cold/catarrh
anginas/tos	a sore throat/cough
un moretón/una ampolla	a bruise/a blister
una quemadura/un sarpullido	a burn/a rash
una picadura	a sting
una intoxicación/una indigestión	food-poisoning/indigestion
Tengo dolor de (estómago)	I have (stomach)-ache
He tenido vómitos	I've been sick
Estoy estreñido	I am constipated
¿Necesito una receta?	Do I need a prescription?

▶ ▶ ▶ **Chemists** These are identified by a green or red cross. Opening hours are the same as other shops but they are usually closed on Saturday afternoons. Each chemist remains open one night a week from 9 to 10 pm and an emergency service is assured by a system of rotas during holidays, at night and at weekends. Look for the duty chemist sign **Farmacia de Guardia**.

en la farmacia/at the chemist's

Luisa has hay-fever and goes to a chemist in Santander.

Luisa: **¿Puede darme algo para la fiebre del heno, por favor?**

Chemist: Sí, señorita. (Hands her a packet of pills) Tiene que tomar un comprimido cada cuatro horas. Son trescientas pesetas.

Luisa: Muchas gracias, adiós.

4 HEALTH AND EMERGENCY

At the chemist's

(*pharmaceutical items and toiletries are listed on p. 81*)

¿Puede darme algo para ...?	Can you give me something for ...?
la fiebre del heno	hay-fever

Tiene que tomar un comprimido/
   la medicina
	You must take a pill/tablet/
	   the medicine

cada cuatro horas/dos veces al día	every 4 hours/twice a day

the way it works

Making polite requests

Note:

¿**Quiere** comprobar el aceite?	Please would you check the oil?
¿**Quiere** arreglar el neumático?	Please would you repair the tyre?
¿**Puede** volver dentro de un rato?	Could you come back in a while?

Reflexive verbs

No **me** siento bien.	I don't feel well	(sentirse = to feel)
... cuando **me** levanto	... when I get up	(levantarse = to get up)

These are examples of verbs being used reflexively, indicating actions done by, to or for oneself. The object of the verb is usually the same as the subject. Reflexive verbs are accompanied by a reflexive pronoun: **me** (myself), **te** (yourself), **se** (him/her/itself), **nos** (ourselves), **os** (yourselves), **se** (themselves):

Me llamo	I am called ...	from llamar**se** (to be called)
Te levantas	You get up	from levantar**se** (to get up)
Se abre	It opens	from abrir**se** (to open)
Nos bañamos	We bathe	from bañar**se** (to bathe)
Se sientan	They sit down	from sentar**se** (to sit down)

Note that the reflexive pronoun comes before the verb unless that verb is in the infinitive or imperative:

Siénte**se**	Sit down! (sentar**se**)	*but*	No **se** preocupe	Don't worry

4 HEALTH AND EMERGENCY

I have a head-ache

Note that when talking about parts of your body you normally use 'the' and not 'a' or 'my' as in English:

Me duele **la** cabeza   I have a head-ache
Abra **la** boca   Open your mouth

How long ago ...?

In Spanish use the phrase: **¿Desde cuándo?** + present tense.

¿Desde cuándo se siente así?   Since when are you feeling thus?

and the reply

Desde hace unos días   Since a few days ago
Hace unos días   A few days ago ('it makes some days').

Hace (it makes) is part of **hacer** (to do or to make). Here is the present tense:

hago	I make	**hacemos**	we make
haces	you make	**hacéis**	you make
hace	he/she/it makes/ you make (formal)	**hacen**	they make/ you make (formal)

things to do

4.3   You are at a petrol station. Tell the attendant in Spanish:

1 to fill the tank up   3 to check the oil
2 that you want 35 litres of 4-star petrol   4 to check the tyre pressures

4.4   Your car has broken down and you are telephoning for help. You say:

1 that your car won't start   3 please could they send a mechanic?
2 that the ignition isn't working   4 how long will that be?

4.5   You are not feeling well. Can you describe your symptoms to the doctor?

Doctor: Buenos días, ¿qué le pasa?
You: [Say your stomach hurts and you have diarrhoea]
Doctor: ¿Desde cuándo se siente así?
You: [For about a week]
Doctor: Bueno, aquí tiene unos comprimidos que deben tomar tres veces al día.
You: [Say thank you and goodbye]

4.6   In the chemist's you are looking for three items:

Chemist: Buenos días, ¿puedo ayudarle?
You: [Ask if she can give you something for insect bites]
Chemist: Aquí tiene. ¿Algo más?
You: [Ask for some sticking plasters and some throat pastilles]

5 ACCOMMODATION

HOTELS AND CAMPSITES

Somewhere to stay There are five official categories of Spanish **hotel**, ranging from the luxurious 5-star downwards. A 3-star hotel will usually offer you your own bathroom. In addition to the top-class hotels there are **paradores**, state-run hotels which are often built in beautiful positions. and sometimes situated in converted palaces and castles.

Less expensive forms of accommodation include the **fonda** (rooms often above an inn), **hostal** (small often family-run hotel graded from 1 to 3 stars), **residencia** (economically priced hotel often without a restaurant), **pensión** (boarding house often containing permanent residents), **albergue** (country inn), and **albergue de juventúd** (youth hostel). The price is for the room and does not vary according to the number of people in it. It does not always include breakfast. Prices of rooms throughout the range are generally cheaper than in Britain. To book a hotel on the spot you can go to the local Tourist Office, but in the tourist season it is essential to book in advance, particularly in the main tourist centres.

Looking for a hotel

¿Dónde hay un hotel? — Where is there a hotel?
¿Hay un hotel cerca de aquí? — Is there a hotel near here?
Busco un buen hotel — I'm looking for a good hotel
   en el centro de la ciudad —   in the city centre

47

5 ACCOMMODATION

ARRIVING AT A HOTEL

¿tiene una habitación doble?/do you have a double room?

Carmen decides to try a hotel recommended by Andrés.

Recepcionista:	Buenos días, señores.
Carmen:	Buenos días. **¿Tiene una habitación doble, por favor?**
Recepcionista:	¿Para cuántas noches?
Carmen:	**Para dos noches**.
Recepcionista:	Bueno … ¿La quiere con baño, señora?
Carmen:	Sí, **con baño si es posible.**
Recepctionista:	Vamos a ver (looks at list) Lo siento, señora. Tenemos habitaciones con lávabo pero no quedan con baño para hoy.
Carmen:	Bueno, no importa. **¿Cuánto es la habitación con lávabo?**
Recepcionista:	Son dos mil quinientas pesetas por noche.
Carmen:	**¿Está incluido el desayuno?**
Recepcionista:	Sí, todo incluido.
Carmen:	Está bien.

Booking a room

Quisiera reservar una habitación.	I'd like to book a room
para mañana/para miércoles	for tomorrow/for Wednesday
Lo siento. Está completo	I'm sorry, it's full up
¿Puede tener una habitación el jueves?	Would you have a room on Thursday?
He reservado una habitación	I have booked a room
¿Hay habitaciones disponibles?	Are there any rooms available?
¿Tiene una habitación disponible?	Do you have a room available?
para esta noche/una noche	for tonight/for one night
para dos/tres noches	for two/three nights
para una semana	for a week
para el miércoles	for Wednesday
para cuatro personas	for four people
Quiero una habitación doble	I want a double room
individual/sencilla	single
con baño/con ducha	with a bathroom/a shower
con lávabo	with a basin
con cama matrimonial/cos camas	with a double bed/twin beds
con un balcón/vista al mar	with a balcony/sea view
Tenemos habitaciones con ducha	We have rooms with a shower
No quedan …	We have none left …
¿Cuál es el precio?	What is the price?
¿Cuánto er por día?	How much is it per day?''
la pensión completa/la media pensión	full board/half board
Es demasiado caro	It is a bit expensive
¿Tiene algo más barato?	Do you have anything cheaper?
¿Está incluido el desayuno?	Is breakfast included?
planta baja	ground floor
primer/segundo/tercer piso	first/second/third-floor

5 ACCOMMODATION

he reservado una habitación/I have booked a room

Andrés and his wife Asunción have booked a room at the same hotel.

Andrés: Buenos días. **He reservado una habitación para dos noches.**

Recepcionista: ¿Cuál es su nombre, por favor?

Andrés: Andrés Valbuena.

Recepcionista: A sí, ... una habitación doble con baño. ¿Quiere llenar esta ficha, señor, y me deja su pasaporte?

Andrés: De acuerdo. (Fills in form)

Recepcionista: Firme aquí, por favor ... Gracias. Su habitación es el número quince en el segundo piso. Aquí tiene su llave.

Andrés: Muchas gracias. **¿Se puede aparcar en la calle?**

Recepcionista: No, en esta calle no se puede, pero hay un aparcamiento detrás del hotel.

At the hotel

He reservado una habitación	I have booked a room
¿Cuál es su nombre?	What is your name?
¿Quiere llenar esta ficha?	Please fill in this form
Me deja su pasaporte	Let me have your passport
su carnet de identidad	your identity card
Es el número quince	It's number 15
en el segundo piso	on the second floor
Aquí tiene su llave	Here is your key
¿Puedo ver la habitación?	Can I see the room?
Esta habitación es demasiado pequeña	This room is too small
¿Me subirá el equipaje?	Will you have the luggage taken up?
¿Se puede aparcar en la calle?	Can one park in the street?
Hay un aparcamiento detrás del hotel	There's a car-park behind the hotel

While you are there ...

Me da la llave, por favor	Please give me my key
No funciona ...	It is not working
el agua caliente/fría	hot water/cold water
la luz/el interruptor de la luz	the light/the light switch
la radio/el televisor	the radio/the television
¿A qué hora es el desayuno?	What time is breakfast?/
la comida?/la cena?	lunch?/dinner?
¿Sirven el desayuno en la habitación?	Do you serve breakfast in the room?

49

5   ACCOMMODATION

Paying the bill

¿Me da la cuenta, por favor?	May I have the bill please?
Creo que hay un error	I think there is a mistake
¿Puedo pagar con cheque?/tarjeta de crédito?	May I pay by cheque/credit card?
¿Está incluido el servicio?	Is service included?

Camping   There are about 350 authorised campsites. Advance booking for popular resorts in the summer is advisable. You can buy a camping guide (**guía de campings**) in most bookshops.

¿hay sitio?/is there a place?

Felipe, a friend of Juan's, arrives with some friends at a campsite near Santander.

Felipe:	Buenas tardes, señor, **¿Hay sitio?**
Guardián:	Sí, hay varios sitios. ¿Cuántas personas son?
Felipe:	**Somos tres. Tengo un coche y una tienda**.
Guardián:	¿Cuántas noches quieren pasar aquí?
Felipe:	**Dos noches, por favor**.
Guardián:	Puede ponerla allí. ¿Quiere llenar esta ficha, por favor?
Felipe:	De acuerdo. **¿Hay duchas calientes?**
Guardián:	Sí, pero no funciona el agua caliente en este momento.
Felipe:	Y ¿hay electricidad?
Guardián:	Sí, ¿quieren toma de corriente?
Felipe:	Sí, por favor.

5 ACCOMMODATION

Prohibido acampar	No camping
¿Hay sitio?	Is there a place?
Hay varios sitios	There are various places
¿Cuántas personas son?	How many are you?
Somos dos	We are two
Tengo una tienda (de campaña)	I have a tent
una caravana	a caravan
Puede ponerla allí	You can put it over there
¿Quiere llenar esta ficha?	Please fill in this form
¿Se puede comprar gas butano?	Can one buy butane gas?
¿Se puede alquilar un saco de dormir?	Can one hire a sleeping-bag?
¿Dónde están las duchas calientes?/	Where are the hot showers?/
los cubos de basura?	the rubbish bins?
¿Dónde está el agua potable?	Where is the drinking water?
No funciona el agua	The water isn't working
los servicios/el retrete	toilets/lavatory
el agua/el grifo	water/tap
la piscina	swimming-pool
¿Hay electricidad?	Is there electricity?
¿Quieren toma de corriente?	Do you want to plug in?
¿Se puede encender una hoguera?	Can one light a bonfire?

the way it works

The Perfect Tense

He reservado una habitación   I have reserved a room

This is an example of the perfect tense, which is used in very much the same way as in English. It is formed with a part of the auxiliary verb **haber** (to have) + a past participle:

he reservado	I have reserved	**hemos** reservado	we have reserved
has reservado	you have reserved	**habéis** reservado	you have reserved
ha reservado	he/she has reserved	**han** reservado	they have reserved
	you have reserved		you have reserved

Note that the past participle **reservado** does not change its ending. Past participles are normally formed by taking the stem of the verb, e.g. **reserv-**, and adding on -ado (-ar verbs), or -ido (-er and -ir verbs).

5   ACCOMMODATION

things to do

5.1   Practise booking different sorts of room at an hotel.

1

2

3

Quiero una habitación . . .

4

5

5.2   You arrive at a hotel having booked a room. Can you fill in your part of the conversation with the receptionist?

You: [Say, good afternoon. You have booked a room]
Recep.:   ¿Su nombre, por favor?
You: [Give your name]
Recep.:   A ver . . . Sí. Una habitación sencilla, número doce. ¿Quiere firmar aquí, por favor? . . . ¿Tiene equipaje?
You: [Say it's in the car]
Recep.:   El botones lo subirá. Aquí tiene su llave.
You: [Thank you very much]

5.3   You want to book a room for the night but you have left it a bit late.

You: [Ask if there is a room free]
Recep.:   Sí. ¿La quiere con baño?
You: [No, say you want a room with a shower].
Recep.:   Sólo tenemos una doble con baño.
You: [Ask how much the room is]
Recep.:   Tres mil seiscientas pesetas por noche.
You: [Say you are sorry but it's too expensive]

5.4   You are making enquiries about a campsite.

You: [Say good afternoon and ask if there is any room]
Guardián: Sí, hay varios sitios. ¿Cuántas personas son?
You: [Say you are four and that you have a caravan]
Guardián: ¿Cuánto tiempo quieren quedarse?
You: [A week]
Guardián: Bueno. Pueden poner la caravana cerca de la playa.

5.5   You are checking up on the facilities of a certain campsite: ¿Hay . . .?

5.6   A lot of things don't seem to be working! Can you tell the warden?

1 the hot showers   2 the toilets   3 the electricity   4 the
tap   5 the drinking water

52

5 RESTAURANTS

ORDERING A MEAL

Restaurants Spanish restaurants are officially classified by forks
(**tenedores**), five being the most, but you can often get a very good meal
in a much more modest establishment such as a **comedor** or a **cafetería**.
Look for the fixed-price menu (**menú del día**) which usually offers three
courses and is often very good value. Cheaper restaurants will often
serve a one-dish meal (**plato combinado**), which combines several
courses on one plate. Service is usually included (**servicio incluido**), but
many people will leave a little extra for really good service.

en el restaurante/in the restaurant

Carmen and Tom have met up with Andrés and his wife Asunción and
they have decided to eat out in a restaurant.

Tom:	**¿Hay una mesa libre?**
Camarero:	¿Para cuántas personas, señor?
Tom:	**Somos cuatro**.
Camarero:	Pasen por aquí, señores. Tengo una mesa cerca de la ventana.

5 RESTAURANTS

(They sit down at the table)

Camarero: ¿Qué van a comer, señores?

Asunción: **Vamos a tomar el menú del día. De primero** quiero el gazpacho andaluz y **de segundo** la chuleta de ternera.

Carmen: **Para mí** los espárragos y el lomo de cerdo.

Andrés: **Yo voy a tomar** la sopa de pescado y el bistec a la parrilla.

Camarero: ¿Cómo prefiere su bistec, señor?

Andrés: **Lo prefiero poco hecho.** (Turns to Tom) ¿Y usted, señor?

Camerero:

Tom: **Pues a mí me gusta mucho** la paella. Voy a tomar la paella y una ensalada mixta.

Camarero: Sí, señor. ¿Y para beber?

Tom: **Tráiganos** una botella de Valdepeñas, y una botella de Chablis.

Carmen: Y una botella de agua mineral, también.

Camarero: En seguida, señores.

(Later the waiter asks them what they want as dessert)

Camarero: ¿Qué quieren **de postre**, señores?

Carmen: Un flan con nata, un helado de vainilla, y una tarta de manzana. **Y la cuenta, también, por favor.**

Ordering a meal

The table

¿Puede recomendar un buen restaurante?	Can you recommend a good restaurant?
Quiero reservar una mesa para las nueve	I want to book a table for nine o'clock
¿Hay una mesa libre?	Is there a free table?
¿Para cuántas personas?	For how many?
Somos cuatro	We are four people
Una mesa para seis, por favor	A table for six, please
Pasen por aquí	Come this way
cerca de la ventana	near the window

The menu

¡Oiga! ¡Camarero!	Waiter!
Tráiga el menú, por favor	The menu please
¿Tiene un menú fijo?	Do you have a set menu?
el menú del día/de la casa	the menu of the day/house menu
el menú gastronómico	the gastronomic menu
¿Qué recomienda hoy?	What do you recommend today?
¿De qué consiste?	What does it consist of?
De primero/de segundo	For first course/second course
gazpacho andaluz	cold tomato soup with cucumber, onions, garlic
chuleta de ternera	veal cutlet
puntas de espárragos	asparagus tips
lomo de cerdo	loin of pork
sopa de pescado	fish soup
bistec a la parrilla	grilled steak
bien hecho, poco hecho	well done, rare

5 RESTAURANTS

paella valenciana	saffron rice and seafood (mussels, shrimps, etc.), with pieces of chicken, peas and peppers
ensalada mixta	mixed salad
¿Quiere algo de postre?	Would you like a dessert?
No, gracias, no quiero nada	No thank you, I don't want anything
flan con nata	caramel custard with cream
helado de vainilla	vanilla ice-cream
tarta de manzana	apple tart

And to drink?

¿Y para beber?	What do you want to drink?
la lista de vinos	the wine-list
Una botella de . . .	A bottle of . . . (see also Unit 1 p. 9)
¿Tiene vino de casa?	Do you have any house wine?
el agua mineral	mineral water
una coca-cola/una cerveza	a coke/a beer
el café para todos	coffee for everyone

The bill

La cuenta, por favor	The bill, please

Meals Breakfast (**el desayuno**) is a light meal consisting usually of coffee and bread or buns. Lunch (**el almuerzo, la comida**) is the main meal of the day and is eaten much later than in Britain, between 2 and 3 pm, followed by a siesta. However, the tradition of a long late lunch is changing in the cities, where you will often find it is eaten earlier, and the siesta is tending to disappear. The evening meal (**la cena**) is also eaten later – at 9 or 10 pm.

en el Hostal Lombraña/at the Hostal Lombraña

Juan meets his friend Felipe and together with Luisa and Miguel they go to a cheap restaurant in town. Juan is taking the orders.

Juan:	¿Qué vais a tomar?
Luisa:	**Para mí, de primero**, sopa de fideos, por favor. Y después una tortilla de jamón con ensalada.
Juan:	¿Y tú, Miguel?
Miguel:	Pues, ¡yo tengo una hambre que me muero! **Voy a tomar** macarrones y albóndigas con salsa de tomate.
Juan:	Y ¿para tí, Felipe?
Felipe:	**Para mí un plato combinado**. Garbanzos y huevos con jamón.
Juan:	Y ¿para beber?
Migue:	Una coca-cola para mí, por favor.
Luisa:	Y para mí un zumo de naranja.

5 RESTAURANTS

Para mí . . .	For me . . .
sopa de fideos	pasta soup
tortilla de jamón con ensalada	ham omelette and salad
(No) tengo hambre	I am (not) hungry
Tengo una hambre que me muero	I am dying of hunger!
Voy a tomar macarrones	I'll have macaroni
albóndigas con salsa de tomate	meat-balls in tomato sauce
garbanzos	chick-peas
huevos con jamón	ham and eggs
(No) tengo sed	I am (not) thirsty

Useful restaurant phrases

pan y cubierto	bread and cover charge
menú turístico	tourist menu
menú del dia	menu of the day
platos combinados	combined dishes
postre a elegir	dessert choice
servicio incluido	service included
sal y pimienta	salt and pepper
Señoras	Ladies
Caballeros	Gentlemen
la mesa	table
la silla	chair
el cuchillo	knife
el tenedor	fork
la cuchara	spoon
el plato	plate, dish
aceite y vinagre	oil and vinegar

❊❊❊ MENÚ DEL DÍA ❊❊❊

gazpacho andaluz	paella valenciana
sopa de pescado	huevos a la flamenca
puntas de espárragos	tortilla de jamón
ensalada mixta	

	flan con nata
chuleta de ternera	helado
lomo de cerdo	tarta de manzana
bistec	fruta del tiempo
conejo al limón	queso

things to do

5.7 Look at this menu and decide what you and your two friends would like to eat: De primero . . ., de segundo . . ., de postre . . .

5.8 Things are not always easy when you try to order a meal . . .

Waiter:	¿Qué va a tomar, señor?
You:	[First, the mussels]
Waiter:	Lo siento, no tenemos hoy.
You:	[Well then, you'll have the fish soup]
Waiter:	Muy bien ¿Y de segundo?
You:	[The hake]
Waiter:	Lo siento, no queda . . .
You:	[Ask if he has a fillet of sole]
Waiter:	Creo que sí, señor. ¿Y de postre?
You:	[An orange, please]
Waiter:	Sólo hay plátanos.
You:	[OK, you'll have a banana and could he bring the bill, please?]

6 SPORT AND LEISURE

TALKING ABOUT SPORTS

¿te gusta el deporte?/do you like sport?

Juan is talking to Miguel about sport.

Juan:	**¿Qué deportes practicas** en Inglaterra?
Miguel:	Pues, en invierno **juego al fútbol** y en verano al tenis. Pero soy muy malo para el tenis – **me gusta más** el fútbol.
Juan:	**A mí me interesa la natación y la pesca**, sobre todo la pesca submarina.
Miguel:	Y **¿sabes hacer** esquí acuático?
Juan:	Sí, **sé hacerlo pero prefiero la natación**. Si te interesa el fútbol, mañana hay un partido en el estadio. **Tienes ganas de** ir?
Miguel:	¡Oh sí! **Me gustaría mucho**. ¿Qué equipos juegan?
Juan:	No sé, pero me parece que es un partido entre el Rácing y el Castellón.
Miguel:	¿A qué hora empieza?
Juan:	**Empieza a las cinco de la tarde**. Bueno, hoy vamos a la taquilla para sacar las entradas.

RESULTADOS CUATRO ÚLTIMAS TEMPORADAS									PRÓXIMO BOLETO	
En el descanso				Domingo 22 de noviembre	Al final del partido				(6 de diciembre)	
83-84	84-85	85-86	86-87		83-84	84-85	85-86	86-87		
1-0	—	1-0	2-0	1 Barcelona-Cádiz............	4-1	—	1-0	2-0	1 Barcelona-Murcia	
0-0	0-0		1-0	2 Murcia-Betis	1-0	0-1	—	3-0	2 Betis-Real Sociedad	
		1-0		3 Real Sociedad-Celta		—	1-1	—	3 Celta-Valladolid	
—	—	—	—	4 Valladolid-Logroñés.......	—	—	—	—	4 Logroñés-Real Madrid	
1-0	—	—	0-0	5 Real Madrid-Mallorca	2-0	—	—	3-0	5 Mallorca-Spórting	
		—	1-0	6 Spórting-Sabadell				2-1	6 Sabadell-Zaragoza	
0-1	1-1	0-0	0-0	7 Zaragoza-At. Madrid	2-2	1-1	0-0	1-0	7 At. Madrid-Osasuna	
1-0	0-2	0-0	0-0	8 Osasuna-Athlétic	1-1	1-2	0-1	0-1	8 Athlétic-Las Palmas	
0-1	—	1-1	0-0	9 Sevilla-Español...........	2-1	0-0	1-1	1-0	9 Valencia-Sevilla	
0-1				10 Castellón-Rácing..........	1-1				10 Cádiz-Español	
		1-0	1-0	11 Sestao-Málaga		—		3-0	11 Rácing-Bilbao Ath.	
0-0		1-1	0-0	12 Recreativo-Elche	1-0		2-1	0-1	12 Burgos-Sestao	
			0-0	13 Jerez-Oviedo			—	0-0	13 Málaga-Recreativo	
0-0	3-2	1-1	0-0	14 Deportivo-Cartagena	3-0	4-2	2-1	1-0	14 Oviedo-Hércules	

A matter of sport

(For a list of sports, see p. 83)

¿Qué deportes practicas?	What sports do you play?
en invierno/en verano	in Winter/in Summer
juego al fútbol, tenis	I play football, tennis
Soy muy malo para ...	I'm very bad at ...
Me gusta más el fútbol	I like football better
No me gusta nada	I don't like it at all
A mí me interesa la natación/ la pesca/la pesca submarina	I'm interested in swimming/ fishing/underwater fishing
¿Sabes hacer esquí acuático?	Do you know how to water-ski?
Sí, sé hacerlo	Yes, I know how to
Prefiero la natación	I prefer swimming
Si te interesa el fútbol	If you are interested in football
Hay un partido	There is a match
en el estadio	in the stadium
¿Tienes ganas de ir?	Would you like to go?
Me gustaría mucho	I'd love to
¿Quiénes juegan?	Who are playing?
Rácing	Santander football team
¿A qué hora empieza?	What time does it begin?
Empieza a las ...	It begins at ...
Vamos a la taquilla ...	Let's go to the ticket office
... para sacar las entradas	... to buy the tickets

Buying tickets

Dos entradas para el partido/ la corrida de mañana	Two tickets for tomorrow's match/bullfight
de tribuna/de general	in the stand/on the terrace
sol/sombra/sol y sombra	in the sun/shade/sun and shade

SIGHTSEEING

6 SPORT AND LEISURE

haciendo turismo/seeing places

Tom and Carmen are in Segovia where they call in at the Oficina de Turismo.

Tom: Buenas tardes. **Quisiera unos folletos sobre la región** y un plano de la ciudad, por favor.

Empleada: Aquí tiene. ¿Algo más?
Tom: **¿Tiene una lista de hoteles?**
Empleada: Claro, señor.
Tom: **¿Sabe a qué hora está abierto el Museo** del Alcázar?
Empleada: Está abierto de nueve a doce y media por la mañana y de tres a siete por la tarde.
Tom: Y **¿cuánto vale la entrada?**
Empleada: Trescientas cincuenta pesetas.
Tom: Muchas gracias, señorita.

Quisiera unos folletos	I'd like some leaflets
un plano de la ciudad	a plan of the city
¿Tiene una lista de hoteles?	Do you have a list of hotels?
¿A qué hora está abierto . . . .?	At what time is the . . . open?
¿A qué hora se abre?	At what time does it open?
¿A qué hora se cierra?	At what time does it close?
¿Cuánto vale la entrada?	How much does a ticket cost?
entrada gratuita	entrance free

Places to see

la catedral	cathedral	el museo	museum
el castillo, el alcázar	castle	el palacio	palace
la cueva	cave	el ayuntamiento	town-hall
la iglesia	church	el parque	park
el claustro	cloister	la plaza de toros	bull-ring
la mezquita	mosque	el monasterio	monastery

the way it works

More verbs with vowel changes

We have already seen some verbs which have a change of vowel in the present tense (see Jueves, por la tarde). We have also seen the following very commonly used verbs:

querer:	to want	} e→ie	quiero	I want
tener:	to have		tienes	you have

6 SPORT AND LEISURE

This stem change occurs usually in the 1st, 2nd and 3rd persons singular and the 3rd person plural. In this unit we have:

empe**z**ar   *to begin*: emp**ie**zo, emp**ie**zas, emp**ie**za, empe**z**amos, empe**z**áis, emp**ie**zan

ce**rr**ar   *to shut*: c**ie**rro, c**ie**rras, c**ie**rra, ce**rr**amos, ce**rr**áis, c**ie**rran

We also have a verb with a different vowel change:

j**u**gar   *to play* u → ue: j**ue**go, j**ue**gas, j**ue**ga, j**u**gamos, j**u**gáis, j**ue**gan

What do you know?

¿**Sabes** hacer esquí acuático? Do you know how to . . .?
Sé hacerlo   I know how to . . .
No **sé**   I don't know

To know something, or to know how to do something in Spanish is **saber**:

sé	I know	**sabemos**	we know
sabes	you know	**sabéis**	you know
sabe	he/she knows	**saben**	they know
	you know (formal)		you know (formal)

However, if you are talking about knowing a person or a place you use the verb **conocer**.

No **conozco** la ciudad   I don't know the city
Encantado de **conocerle**   Pleased to meet you

Note that when talking about knowing a person, you insert **a** before that person.

Conocen a muchos ingleses   They know many English people

Here is the present tense:

conozco	I know	**conocemos**	we know
conoces	you know	**conocéis**	you know
conoce	he/she knows	**conocen**	they know
	you know (formal)		you know (formal)

Question words

Here is a list of some of the question words from the dialogues in this unit and elsewhere:

¿**Qué**?	What?	¿**Qué** deportes practicas?
¿**Quién**?/¿**Quiénes**?	Who?	¿**Quiénes** juegan?
¿**Cuándo**?	When?	¿**Cuándo** empieza?
¿**Cuánto**?	How much?	¿**Cuánto** vale la entrada?
¿**Cuántos/as**?	How many?	¿**Cuántas** personas son?
¿**Cuál**?	Which?	¿**Cuál** es su nombre?
¿**Cómo**?	How?	¿**Cómo** te llamas? (literally, How are you called?)
		¿**Cómo** es? (literally, How is it?)

Note that question-words always carry a written accent.

6 SPORT AND LEISURE

things to do

6.1 You are being asked what sports you play.

Interviewer: ¿Qué deportes practicas?
You: [Say you play tennis and you like swimming]
Interviewer: ¿Te gusta también el fútbol?
You: [Say you don't like it at all]
Interviewer: ¿Sabes jugar al golf?
You: [Yes, you know how to but you prefer tennis]

6.2 ¿Te gusta el deporte? Me gusta .../No me gusta .../Soy muy malo para ...

1 Luisa likes ball-games but hates water-sports. When asked what sports she likes, what does she say?
2 Juan likes most things to do with water, but is no good at ball-games. When asked which sports he likes what does he say?
3 Now can you say what sports or games you like, what you don't like and what you are bad at?

6.3 Felipe takes Luisa to see the Tito Bustillo cave, where they talk to the empleada, the assistant.

Felipe: [Two tickets, please]
Empleada: [Say how much two cost]
Felipe: [Ask what time they open]
Empleada: [Say they open at 3 pm]
He also takes her to the Claustro Romano.
Felipe: [Two tickets, please]
Empleada: [Say how much two cost]
Felipe: [Ask what time it closes]
Empleada: [Say it closes at 7 pm]

6.4 Can you match the following questions and answers?

1 ¿Te gusta la equitación?   (a) Sí, sé hacerlo.
2 ¿Qué equipo juega?   (b) Prefiero la pesca.
3 ¿Prefieres la pesca o la natación? (c) De nueve a doce.
4 ¿Sabes jugar ajedrez (chess)?   (d) No, no me gusta nada.
5 ¿A qué hora está abierta?   (e) Juega el equipo de
                                         Salamanca.

6.5 You are introduced to señor Santillana at a party (una reunión) and fall into conversation with him. Can you ask these questions in Spanish?

1 Ask him if he knows Victor, a colleague from your office in London?
   ¿Conoces a Victor, un colega de mi oficina en Londres?
2 Ask if he knows Conchita, a friend of your wife?
3 Does he know how to play chess?
4 Ask him if he knows when the party finishes? (use *se termina*)
5 Say you know your wife would like to meet him.

6 SPORT AND LEISURE

MAKING PLANS

las vacaciones/holidays

Carmen talks to a student about his holiday plans.

Carmen: ¿Cuándo piensas ir de vacaciones este año?
Estudiante: Pues, **pienso ir a principios de septiembre**.
Carmen: ¿Adónde piensas ir? Al extranjero, a las montañas, al mar?
Estudiante: Este **año voy a Cantabria** – primero a Santander.
Carmen: Y ¿qué vas a hacer allí?
Estudiante: Voy a alquilar un coche y **visitaré muchos sitios**. Tengo
ganas de ver los Picos de Europa.
Carmen: ¿Cuánto tiempo te quedarás en Asturias?
Estudiante: **Me quedaré unos quince días**, o sea, **volveré a mi casa**
dentro de tres semanas, nada más. Estoy estudiando
idiomas y vuelvo a clase el 21 de septiembre.

Holidays

¿Cuándo piensas ir ...?	When do you think you'll go ...?
... de vacaciones?	... on holiday?
Pienso ir	I'm thinking of going
a principios de	at the beginning of
a finales de	at the end of
septiembre	September (for months see p. 79)
¿Adónde piensas ir?	Where are you thinking of going?
al extranjero	abroad
a las montañas/al mar	to the mountains/to the sea
primero	firstly
Voy a alquilar un coche	I'm going to hire a car

visitaré muchos sitios	I will visit many places
Tengo ganas de ver ...	I feel like seeing ...
los Picos de Europa	the Asturian mountains
¿Cuánto tiempo te quedarás?	How long will you stay?
Me quedaré unos quince días	I shall stay about a fortnight
Volveré dentro de tres semanas	I shall return within three weeks
Estoy estudiando idiomas	I'm studying languages
vuelvo a clase	I go back to my classes

Dates

¿En qué fecha estamos?	What's the date today?
el primero de mayo	1st of May
el cuatro de abril	2nd of April
el veintiuno de septiembre	21st of September
sábado, diez de octubre	Saturday the 10th of October
el mes pasado	last month
la semana próxima	next week
este año	this year
el cumpleaños	birthday
Navidad/Pascua	Christmas/Easter
ayer/hoy/mañana	yesterday/today/tomorrow
abierto/cerrado	open/shut
todos los días	every day
(días) laborables	working days
(días) festivos	public holidays, feast-days

GOING TO THE CINEMA

Going to the cinema In the city, cinemas generally have three showings: one at about 4.30 pm, the next at about 7.30 pm, and the last at about 10 or 11 pm. You may find a continuous session (**sesión continua**) starting at about 4 or 5 pm. In the country, there may only be two sessions (**función de la tarde** and **función de la noche**). Many foreign films are shown and most are dubbed into Spanish. Where they are shown in the original language with subtitles this is indicated by **V.O.** (**subtituladas**). It is customary to tip the usher (**acomodador/a**).

SESIÓN CONTINUA

Cristal. (2) / ☎ 234 93 53 / Bravo Murillo, 120; Cuatro Caminos / *Metro* Cuatro Caminos.
—**Luna de lobos y Superedetective en Hollywood II.** No recomendadas para menores de 13 años. Continua desde las 4.35 de la tarde.
España. (3) / ☎ 269 56 70 / General Ricardos, 4 / *Metro* Marqués de Vadillo. Autobús 34.
—**Cuenta conmigo y Nadine.** Toleradas. 4.30.
Espronceda. (4) / ☎ 441 92 51 / Alonso Cano, 28; Chamberi / *Metro* Ríos Rosas.
—**Las nuevas aventuras de Popeye y Superman IV.** Laborables, continua, 5; sábados y festivos, 4.30. Toleradas.
Europa. (3) / ☎ 233 10 48 / Bravo Murillo, 160; Tetuán / *Metro* Estrecho.

6 ENTERTAINMENT

¿qué te gustaría hacer?/what would you like to do?

Felipe invites Luisa to go out with him but they don't know where to go . . .

Felipe: ¿Qué vamos a hacer esta noche?
Luisa: Pues, no sé. ¿Te gustaría ir a una discoteca?
Felipe: No, bailar no me gusta nada.
Luisa: Entonces ¿qué te gusta hacer en tu tiempo libre?
Felipe: **Me gusta ir al cine**, salir con amigos, escuchar musica . . . Y tú, ¿cuáles son tus aficiones?
Luisa: No sé . . . Me gusta bailar, me gusta mucho ir al teatro, y me gusta escuchar música. Me encanta la música pop.
Felipe: Esa no me gusta. **Prefiero la música clásica**. Toco el piano y estoy aprendiendo la flauta.
Luisa: Pues, mira, ¿**por qué no vamos al cine**?
Felipe: Buena idea. ¿Sabes qué películas ponen en este moment?
Luisa: No. Hay que mirar la cartelera.

Going out or staying in?

¿Qué te gusta hacer?	What do you like doing?
¿Qué vamos a hacer?	What shall we do?
¿Te gustaría ir a . . .?	Would you like to go to . . .?
¿Qué te parece ir a . . .?	What do you think of going to . . .?
No puedo salir esta tarde	I can't go out this evening
Buena idea	Good idea
Me gustaría mucho	I should like to very much
Me encantaría	I should love to
Bailar no me gusta nada	I don't like dancing at all
tu tiempo libre	your free time
Me gusta . . .	I like . . .
ir al cine/al teatro	going to the cinema/theatre
salir con amigos	going out with friends
ir a los toros	go to a bullfight
escuchar música	listening to music
bailar	dancing
pasear/dar paseos	going for walks
ver la televisión	watching television
leer	reading
¿Cuáles son tus aficiones?	What are your hobbies?
Es difícil	It's difficult

Listening to or playing music

Me encanta . . .	I adore . . .
la música pop	pop music

6 ENTERTAINMENT

la música clásica	classical music
ir a un concierto	going to a concert
la orquesta/el cantador	orchestra/singer
Toco el piano/la flauta/el violín/ el clarinete/la trompeta/la guitarra	I play the piano/flute/violin/ the clarinet/trumpet/guitar
Estoy aprendiendo	I am learning

Going to the cinema

¿Por qué no vamos al cine?	Why don't we go to the cinema?
una película	film
¿qué películas ponen?	what films are showing?
en este momento	at the moment
V.O. subtitulada	with subtitles
sesión continua	continuous performance
Autorizada para todos los públicos	Suitable for everyone
No recomendada para menores de 18 años	Not recommended for under 18's
Hay que mirar la cartelera	We'll have to look in the entertainments page

Buying a ticket for a show

la taquilla	box office
asientos limitos	limited seating
la butaca/el anfiteatro	stalls/circle
¿Hay localidades para esta función?	Are there seats for this performance?
Localidades desde 250 pesetas	Seats from 250 pesetas
Dos entradas, por favor	Two tickets, please
¿A qué hora empieza el espectáculo?	What time does the show start?
¿Hay descuentos para estudiantes?	Are there student discounts?
la localidad, la entrada	ticket
venta anticipada	tickets in advance

the way it works

I'm learning the flute

| Estoy estudiando | I am studying |
| Estoy aprendiendo | I am learning |

It's useful to be able to use the continuous present tense which is formed in a similar way to the English 'I am . . .ing'.
Use the present tense of **estar + present participle**, which is formed by taking the stem of the verb:

| **escuch-** and adding **-ando** | for -ar verbs |
| **aprend-** and adding **-iendo** | for -er and -ir verbs |

The future tense

Visitaré muchos sitios	I shall visit many places
Me quedaré quince días	I shall stay a fortnight
Volveré a mi casa	I shall come home

6 · ENTERTAINMENT

These are examples of the future tense which is used as an alternative to
ir + infinitive: **Voy a** alquilar un coche   I'm going to hire a car

The future tense is formed normally by taking the infinitive and adding the following
endings:

visitar-**é**	I shall visit	visitar-**emos**	we shall visit
visitar-**ás**	you will visit	visitar-**éis**	you will visit
visitar-**á**	he/she will visit	visitar-**án**	they will visit
	you will visit (formal)		you will visit (formal)

These endings are the same for all verbs but some verbs form the future stem from
a variation of the infinitive. Some common examples are:

salir:	to go out	sal**dré**	I shall go out
tener:	to have	ten**dré**	I shall have
hay	there is	ha**brá**	There will be

things to do

6.6   ¿**Cuáles son tus aficiones?** What do you like doing in your spare time?

Me encanta   me gusta mucho   me gusta   no me gusta nada

En casa	*Por la tarde*	*De vacaciones*
1 ver la televisión	salir con amigos	ir a las montañas
2 jugar a las cartas	ir al cine	ir a la playa
3 leer	ir al teatro	visitar muchos sitios
4 escuchar la música	ir a un restaurante	hacer el esquí
5 cocinar (to cook)	ir a una discoteca	ir al extranjero

6.7   1   What is being advertised here?
2   What does the advert say about
César Delgado and Teresa del Sol?
3   What days of the week is it open?
4   What times of day?
5   Where is the exhibition held?

> ## GALERÍAS
> ## DE ARTE
> **EXPOSICIONES**
> **Ateneo de Madrid.** Sala de exposiciones
> Santa Catalina / Santa Catalina, 10.
> —Exposición de **César Delgado,** pintor, y **Te-
> resa del Sol,** ceramista. De lunes a sábados,
> de 18 a 20 horas.

la exposición   exhibition
la ceramista   ceramic artist

6.8   You want to buy tickets for a theatre performance.

1   Ask if there are any tickets
for tonight.
2   Ask the price of the tickets.

3   Say you would like two tickets.
4   Ask how much it comes to.
5   Ask what time the show starts.

7 SOCIAL MATTERS

MAKING A PHONE CALL

You can telephone direct to Britain from all big cities and towns and most tourist centres. Look for a telephone box (**cabina telefónica**) marked **Teléfono Internacional**. To call the UK, lift the receiver, wait for the dialling tone, dial 07, wait for a higher tone, dial 44 followed by the UK STD code (without the initial 0) and then the number.

una llamada telefónica/a telephone call

Luisa suggests it might be a good idea to telephone Pilar to let her know when they are returning to Madrid.

Luisa:	¿Oye, Juan, vas a llamar a tu madre?
Juan:	Sí, sí, la llamaré ahora mismo.
Luisa:	**¿Cuál es tu número?** Voy a marcarlo si quieres.
Juan:	Es el 33-78-92.
Luisa:	(dials the number) Aquí tienes. (Juan takes over.)
Pilar:	**Diga.**
Juan:	**Hola mamá. Soy yo, Juan.** ¿Qué tal?
Pilar:	Hola. ¿Qué hay? ¿Qué tal Luisa y Miguel? ¿Qué estáis haciendo? ¿Cuándo vais a volver a Madrid?

7 SOCIAL MATTERS

Juan: Pues, estamos muy bien ... Llegamos el miércoles por la tarde, ... el jueves Luisa y Miguel se dieron una vuelta por Santander y compraron unas cosas. ... El sábado yo fui con Miguel a un partido de fútbol y Luisa fue en coche con un amigo mío a ... algún sitio. ¿Adónde fuiste, Luisa?

Luisa: A muchos sitios – a Cangas de Onís y ...

Juan: (to Pilar) Fueron a Cangas de Onís. Y por la noche se fueron al cine. En fin, lo estamos pasando muy bien.

Pilar: ¿Con quién salió Luisa? ¿Con Martín?

Juan: No ... con Felipe. Es un buen chico, sabes, muy serio.

Pilar: ¡Ah, sí! Me acuerdo ... Bueno, y ¿cuándo pensáis volver?

Juan: A lo mejor, mañana. Cogeremos el tren de las once y media y llegaremos a eso de las seis de la tarde.

Pilar: Muy bien. Entonces, hasta mañana.

Juan: **Adiós, mamá.**

Telephone talk

llamar por teléfono	to telephone
¿Cuál es tu/su número?	What's your number?
Mi número de teléfono es ...	My number is ...
Quiero hablar con	I want to speak to ...
marcar	to dial
Diga, Dígame	Hello (when picking up receiver)
¿Quién habla?	Who's speaking?
¿De parte de quién?	Who's calling?
Llamo de parte de ...	I'm speaking on behalf of ...
Soy ...	It's ... (+ speaker's name)
Hable más despacio/lento	Speak more slowly
No entiendo	I don't understand
¿Quiere dejarle algún recado?	Do you want to leave him a message?
¿Quiere decirle que ...	Please tell him that ...
la guía telefónica	telephone directory
el teléfono internacional	international telephone box
el prefijo	area code
el cobro revertido	reverse charge call

Saying what you did

Llegamos el miércoles	We arrived on Wednesday
se dieron una vuelta por Santander	they walked around Santander
compraron unas cosas	they bought some things
yo fui a un partido de fútbol	I went to a football match

7 SOCIAL MATTERS

Carmen fue en coche a ...	Carmen drove to ...
algún sitio	some place
¿Adónde fuisteis?	Where did you go?
Fuimos a Cangas de Onís	We went to Cangas de Onís
se fueron al cine	they went to the cinema
¿Con quién salió Luisa?	Who did Luisa go out with?
Un buen chico, muy serio	A good lad, very serious
Sí, me acuerdo	Yes, I remember

the way it works

Saying what you are doing

¿Qué estáis haciendo?	What are you doing?
Lo estamos pasando muy bien	We are having a good time

Saying what you intend to do

le llamaré ahora mismo	I'll ring her at once
¿Cuándo pensáis volver?	When do you intend to come back?
A lo mejor, mañana	Probably tomorrow
Cogeremos el tren	We'll catch the train
Llegaremos a eso de las seis	We'll arrive about six

Saying what happened

Fui a un partido de fútbol	I went to a football match.
¿Adónde **fuiste?**	Where did you go?

llegamos (we arrived), **pasearon** (they walked around), **compraron** (they bought), **salió** (she went out).

All these verbs are in the **preterite** tense, which is used a great deal in Spanish for relating past events. The endings for this tense are as follows:

-ar verbs, e.g. **comprar** (to buy)

compr**é**	I bought	compr**amos**	we bought
compr**aste**	you bought (fam.)	compr**asteis**	you bought (fam.)
compr**ó**	he/she/you bought	compr**aron**	they/you bought

-er verbs, e.g. **volver** (to return)

volv**í**	I returned	volv**imos**	we returned
volv**iste**	you returned (fam.)	volv**isteis**	you returned (fam.)
volv**ió**	he/she/you returned	volv**ieron**	they/you returned

-ir verbs, e.g. **salir** (to leave)

sal**í**	I left	sal**imos**	we left
sal**iste**	you left (fam.)	sal**isteis**	you left (fam.)
sal**ió**	he/she/you left	sal**ieron**	they/you left

7 SOCIAL MATTERS

A number of verbs are irregular in the preterite. Here are three common ones:

dar (to give)

di	I gave	**dimos**	we gave
diste	you gave	**disteis**	you gave
dio	he/she gave, you gave	**dieron**	they gave, you gave

ir (to go) *and* **ser** (to be) (**ir** and **ser** share the same pattern)

fui	I went	**fuimos**	we went
fuiste	you went (fam.)	**fuisteis**	you went
fue	he/she/you went	**fueron**	they went/you went

hacer (to do, make)

hice	I made	**hicimos**	we made
hiciste	you made	**hicisteis**	you made
hizo	he/she/it made, you made	**hicieron**	they made/you made

Some verbs have a change in the spelling to enable them to keep the same stem sound throughout: **llegar** (to arrive) **llegué** (I arrived)

things to do

7.1 You are being interviewed about your daily routine.

Interviewer:	¿A qué hora se levanta?
You:	(I get up at 7.30)
Interviewer:	¿Y qué hace después?
You:	(I have my breakfast) (use desayunarse)
Interviewer:	¿A qué hora sale de la casa?
You:	(I Leave at 9.00 and catch the bus to my office)
Interviewer:	¿Vuelve a casa para almorzar? (to have lunch)
You:	(Yes, I come home at midday and have lunch. Then I do my shopping (voy de compras) and go back to the office in the afternoon)

7.2 The interviewer now wants to know what you did last Tuesday. Use the phrases from the previous exercise and put the verbs into the past tense:

Interviewer:	El martes, ¿a qué hora se levantó?	You:	....
Interviewer:	Y ¿qué hizo después?	You:	....
Interviewer:	¿A qué hora salió de la casa?	You:	....
Interviewer:	¿Volvió a casa para almorzar?	You:	....
Interviewer:	¿Qué hizo después?	You:	....

7.3 Using the telephone. The telephone rings and you pick up the receiver. Can you take your part in a telephone conversation in which arrangements are being made.

You:	[Hello]
Juan:	Hola, soy Juan. ¿Qué hay? Oye, quisiera invitarte a cenar esta tarde. Hoy es nuestra última noche en Santander, – y mañana volvemos a Madrid.
You:	[Say you'd like to very much. Ask what time to come]
Juan:	Pues, a eso de las ocho. ¿Sabes dónde estamos?
You:	[Say, yes, you know where he lives and you'll take a taxi]
Juan:	Bueno, entonces, hasta la vista.

DESCRIBING PEOPLE/THINGS

¿puede decirme cómo eran?/can you tell me what were they like?

Carmen has been asked to give a description of a couple she saw shoplifting.

Policía:	¿Cómo eran, por favor?
Carmen:	Pues. mira, **eran un chico y una chica**. El chico tenía unos veinte años, y la chica unos veinticinco.
Policía:	**¿La chica era rubia o morena?**
Carmen:	**Era rubia y bastante baja. Tenía los ojos azules** y el pelo largo y rubio.
Policía:	Y ¿qué llevaba?
Carmen:	Llevaba una falda negra muy corta, y un jersey verde.
Policía:	¿Y el chico?
Carmen:	Era muy alto y moreno. **Llevaba vaqueros y botas** y una chaqueta de cuero.
Policía:	Muy bien. ¿Y a qué distancia de ellos estaba usted?
Carmen:	Estaba a unos tres metros, nada más.
Policía:	¿Qué estaban haciendo?
Carmen:	Metían unos objetos en un bolso y de repente me vieron. Al verme salieron corriendo.

Describing what you saw

¿Cómo eran?	What were they like?
eran un chico y una chica	There were a boy and a girl
tenía unos veinte años	he was about 20
tenía unos veinticinco	she was about 25
¿era rubia o morena?	was she fair or dark?
bastante baja	quite short
tenía los ojos azules	she had blue eyes
el pelo largo	long hair
¿Qué llevaba?	What was she wearing?
alto y moreno	tall and dark
llevaba vaqueros	he was wearing jeans
¿A qué distancia de ellos estaba?	What distance away were you?
estaba a unos tres metros	I was about 3 metres away
Metían unos objetos	They were putting some things
en un bolso ...	in a bag ...
de repente me vieron	they suddenly caught sight of me
Al verme se escaparon	As soon as they saw me they fled
sin esperarse	in a flash

SAYING GOODBYE

hasta el año que viene/see you next year

Juan's party is in full swing and everyone is enjoying themselves. They are out in the garden after supper.

Luisa: ¡Qué noche más estupenda! Lo hemos pasado muy bien aquí en España.

Felipe: **Siento mucho que no puedas quedarte en Santander**. ¿Pero volverás el año próximo, me prometes?

Luisa: Seguramente.

Felipe: ¿Qué cosas te gustan más en España?

Luisa: Pues, no hay problema. Me encanta el buen tiempo, que la gente es muy simpática, y **todo el mundo se divierte** mucho.

Felipe: Sí, es verdad. Pero, ¿qué pasa? ¡**Está lloviendo**! Y el pronóstico para mañana es malo – habrá tormentas. Eso no puede ser . . .

(They go inside, where Juan is being a good host)

Juan: Hola, Felipe. ¿Quieres otra bebida?

Felipe: No, gracias, ya es tarde y tengo que irme. Oye, Juan, ¿por qué no vamos a Inglaterra en la primavera?

Juan: Me gustaría mucho. ¿Estarás en Madrid la semana próxima, ¿verdad?

Felipe: Claro que sí. Bueno, pues te veré en Madrid. Muchas gracias y adiós a todos.

Juan: Adiós, hasta luego.

Party conversation

¡Qué noche más estupenda!	What a lovely evening!
Lo hemos pasado muy bien	We have really enjoyed ourselves
Siento mucho que no puedas quedarte	I'm sorry you can't stay
Volverás el año próximo	You'll come back next year
¿me prometes?	you promise me?
seguramente/no hay problema	certainly/no problem
Hace buen tiempo	It's good weather
todos los días	every day
la gente es muy simpática	people are nice
todo el mundo se divierte	everyone enjoys themselves
Sí, es verdad	Yes, it's true
¿Qué pasa?	What's happening?
Está lloviendo	It's raining
El pronóstico para mañana	The forecast for tomorrow
habrá tormentas	there will be thunderstorms
Eso no puede ser	That's not possible!

7 SOCIAL MATTERS

¿Quieres otra bebida?	Do you want another drink?
Tengo que irme	I have to go
¿Por qué no vamos a Inglaterra?	Why don't we go to England?
en la primavera	in the Spring
Te veré en Madrid, ¿verdad?	I'll see you in Madrid, won't I?
Claro que sí	Certainly
Muchas gracias y adiós	Many thanks and goodbye
Adiós, hasta luego	Goodbye, till then

The weather (El tiempo)

¿Que tiempo hace?	What's the weather like?
Hace sol/Habrá sol	It's sunny/there will be sunshine
Hace frío/viento	It's cold/windy
Hace buen/mal tiempo	It's fine weather/bad weather
Está nublado	It's cloudy
Está lloviendo/nevando	It's raining/snowing
Habrá temporal/tormenta	There will be a gale/storm
el cielo nuboso/cubierto	cloudy/overcast sky
el cielo despejado	clear sky
la lluvia/el chubasco	rain/shower
la nieve/el granizo/la niebla	snow/hail/fog
la borrasca/el anticiclón	depression/anticyclone

the way it works

Saying what someone was like

Tenía unos veinte años	He was about 20.
Era rubia y bastante baja	She was fair and quite short.
Estaba a unos tres metros	I was about 3 metres away

These are examples of the **imperfect** tense. This tense is mainly used for past descriptions of people and places, for saying what you or someone else were doing, or what was happening. It is usually formed by taking the stem of the verb and adding on endings as follows:

-ar verbs e.g. **llevar** (to wear, carry)

llev-**aba**	I was wearing	llev-**ábamos**	we were wearing
llev-**abas**	you were wearing	llev-**abais**	you were wearing
llev-**aba**	he/she was wearing	llev-**aban**	they were wearing
	you were wearing		you were wearing

-er and -ir verbs share the same endings

ten-**ía**	I had	ten-**íamos**	we had
ten-**ías**	you had	ten-**íais**	you had
ten-**ía**	he/she had, you had	ten-**ían**	they had, you had

7 SOCIAL MATTERS

A handful of verbs form the imperfect differently, among them **ser** (to be).

era	I was	**éramos**	we were
eras	you were	**erais**	you were
era	he/she was, you were	**eran**	they were, you were

The imperfect is often used in conjunction with the preterite when two things are happening at the same time: **Metían** unos objetos en un bolso cuando me **vieron**. (They were putting some things in a bag when they caught sight of me.)

Al verme ...

Al verme se escaparon   On seeing me they fled

The use of **al + infinitive** is very common to join two verbs with the same subject: **Al acabar** sus estudios volvió a Madrid. (On finishing her studies she returned to Madrid.)

The weather is terrific!

Hace muy bien tiempo   It's lovely weather

Hace comes from **hacer** (to make) and is often used when talking about the weather. (See Jueves Part 2 for present tense)

It's sunny every day!

todos los días   every day   **todo el** mundo   everyone

To say 'all' or 'every' use **todo, toda, todos, todas**.

Really and truly

verdaderamente   really   seguramente   surely   súbitamente   suddenly

To form an adverb you normally add **-mente** on to the feminine form of the adjective. Other common adverbs include:

desgraciadamente   unluckily   afortunadamente   fortunately

things to do

7.4   What were you doing in Madrid? Some time ago you were living there and you are now being interviewed about it.

Interviewer:	¿Qué hacías en Madrid?
You:	[Say you were studying Spanish]
Interviewer:	Dónde vivías?
You:	[Say you were living in the Calle de Serrano with a family]
Interviewer:	¿Había unos hijos en la familia?
You:	[Yes, there was a daughter]
Interviewer:	¿Cómo se llamaba la hija y cuántos años tenía?
You:	[She was called Mari-Carmen and she was 23]

7 SOCIAL MATTERS

Interviewer:	¿Qué hacías por la tarde?
You:	[You went out with friends, or sometimes you stayed at home and read, or watched television]
Interviewer:	En fin, ¿te gustaba Madrid]
You:	[Say yes, you liked it very much and you had a wonderful time]

.5 Miguel thinks he has lost his watch and he goes to the police station to report it. Look at the following interview and see if you can understand it:

Miguel:	Buenas tardes. Creo que he perdido mi reloj en la calle.
Policía:	¿Cuándo lo perdió, señor?
Miguel:	Pues, esta tarde fui al partido de fútbol y estoy seguro de que lo llevaba cuando salí del estadio.
Policía:	Sí, señor, pero ¿cuándo se dió usted cuenta de que lo había perdido?
Miguel:	Al llegar a mi casa me di cuenta de que no lo tenía. Lo busqué por todas partes pero no lo encontré.
Policía:	¿El reloj era de gran valor, señor?
Miguel:	Pues, no sé exactamente, pero mi abuela me lo dió como regalo.
Policía:	Bueno, ... Quiere llenar este formulario, por favor, con todos los detalles y veremos ... ¿Vive aquí en Santander?
Miguel:	No, mañana vuelvo a Madrid.

The language of losing something

perder	to lose	**He perdido**	I have lost
robar	to steal	**Me han robado**	Someone has stolen
buscar	to look for	**Busqué**	I looked
encontrar	to find	**No encontré**	I didn't find
darse cuenta	to realise	**Me di cuenta**	I realised
el reloj	watch	**la cartera**	wallet
la bolsa	handbag	**la cámara**	camera

Now try to report what Miguel said, with the help of the following phrases:
Esta tarde, Miguel ... a un partido de fútbol y ... seguro de que lo ... cuando ... del estadio. A llegar a su casa ... cuenta de que no lo ... Lo ... por todas partes pero no lo ... .

7 SOCIAL MATTERS

7.6 **El pronóstico para mañana** (The forecast for tomorrow – showing that the weather in Spain isn't always idyllic!)

Cantábrico. Cielo muy nuboso o cubierto con chubascos, que serán en forma de nieve an altitudes superior a los 1.000 metros. Los vientos serán fuertes del Noroeste. Habrá temporal fuerte con mar arbolada en la zona marítima. Máximas de 6° y mínimas de −5°.

1 Will the sky be clear or cloudy?
2 Will the showers be of rain or snow?
3 What direction will the winds be from?
4 Where will there be a gale?
5 What will be the minimum temperature?

7.7 **¿Qué tiempo hace?** Here is a weather map of Spain. Can you say what the weather is like:

1 en el mar mediterráneo?
2 en los pirineos?
3 en Madrid?
4 en el sur de España?
5 en el noroeste?

ANSWER KEY

1.1 1 Buenas días, señora. ¿Cómo está usted? 2 Buenas tardes, señor. ¿Cómo está? 3 Hola, ¿cómo estás?/Muy bien, gracias. 4 Hola, buenas tardes, ¿qué tal?

1.2 Sí, soy Annie Rogers./Sí, este es mi hermano, Felipe./Sí, es mi maleta./Sí, es su maleta.

1.3 1 ¿Es usted la señora Barillo? 2 ¿Es esta su maleta? 3 ¿Dónde está? 4 ¿Cómo está usted? 5 ¿Cómo se llama su hermana?

1.4 (Personal preferences).

1.5 Thomas: un tinto, por favor. Alice: una coca-cola, por favor. Isabel: una taza de té con limón, por favor. Martin: Yo quiero una cerveza, por favor. You:

1.6 ¿Qué bocadillos hay?/Uno de jamón, por favor. ¿Qué helados hay?/Uno de fresa, por favor.

1.7 1 (c). 2 (e). 3 (d). 4 (a). 5 (b).

2.1 1 (d). 2 (f). 3 (a). 4 (e). 5 (b). 6 (c).

2.2 1 Yo también hablo el inglés. 2 Yo también estudio idiomas. 3 Yo también trabajo en Londres. 4 Nosotros también hablamos el español. 5 Nosotros también estudiamos el español.

2.3 1 Se llama Eduardo. Es español de Madrid. Es contable. Tiene veinticuatro años. Es bajo y gordo. Tiene un hermano.

2.4 1 Yo vivo en Madrid. ¿Dónde vive usted? 2 Yo vivo en Tarragona, pero mi hermano vive en Valencia. 3 Nosotros vivimos en Toledo. ¿Dónde vive usted? 4 Y ellos, ¿dónde viven? ¿En Salamanca? No, viven en Ciudad Real.

2.5 1 Son las cuatro. 2 Son las cuatro y cuarto. 3 Son las cuatro y veinte. 4 Son las cuatro y diez. 5 Son las cinco menos cuarto. 6 Son las cinco menos veinte. Son las tres y media. Son las cinco menos veinticinco.

2.6 1 Hay uno a las once veinticinco. 2 Hay uno a las quince treinta. 3 Hay uno a las cinco cuarenta y cinco. 4 Hay uno a las nueve treinta. 5 Hay uno a las diez treinta y cinco.

2.7 1 Son tres mil setecientas pesetas. 2 Son siete mil quinientas pesetas. 3 Son cuatro mil doscientas pesetas.

2.8 1 ¿A qué hora sale el próximo tren para Sevilla?/¿A qué hora llega a Sevilla? 2 Uno, por favor. ¿Qué línea es para Colón?/¿Tengo que hacer transbordo?

3.1 2 Sí, es verde. 3 No, es blanca. Es de algodón. 4 No, es azúl. Es de lana. 5 Sí, son grises.

3.2 Quisiera una camiseta./La cuarenta./Me gusta el estilo pero no me gusta el color./Me gusta más la azúl. ¿Puedo probármela?/Me parece bien. ¿Cuánto es, por favor?/Bueno, la compro.

3.3 1 No, es demasiado pequeño. ¿Hay otro más grande?/2 No, es demasiado larga. ¿Hay otra más corta?/ 3 No, es demasiado grande. ¿Hay otro más pequeño?/4 Son demasiado cortos. ¿Hay otros más largos? 5 Son demasiado pequeños. ¿Hay otros más grandes?

3.4 Belt: dos mil setecientas pesetas. Handbag: nueve mil doscientas pesetas. Guitar: seis mil quinientas pesetas. Porrón: ochocientas pesetas. Necklace: doce mil seiscientas pesetas.

3.5 1 (c). 2 (f). 3 (d). 4 (b). 5 (a). 6 (e).

3.6 1 (e). 2 (h). 3 (d). 4 (g). 5 (b). 6 (c). 7 (f). 8 (a).

3.7 250 gramos de mantequilla; 1 litro de leche; 500 gramos de jamón de York; 1 paquete de galletas; 1 lata de sardinas; 1 kilo de plátanos; ½ kilo de melocotones, 6 peras maduras; 1 litro de aceite; 2 botellas de vino tinto; 12 huevos.

3.8 el café: ciento noventa ptas; 12 huevos: ciento noventa ptas; los plátanos: cien ptas; los tomates: trescientas ptas. Total: setecientas ochente ptas.

3.9 Doscientos gramos de queso y cien gramos de jamón serrano, por favor./medio kilo de manzanas y seis plátanos maduros./Un litro de leche, por favor. Eso es todo. ¿Cuánto es, por favor?

3.10 Buenos días, quisiera cambiar unas libras esterlinas, por favor./Ciento cincuenta libras. ¿A cómo es el cambio hoy?/Deme seis billetes de cinco mil pesetas, por favor.

3.11 Quiero dos de estos pasteles y una tarta, por favor./Sí, deme un donut y un panecillo/No, es para llevar.

ANSWER KEY

4.1 Tome la primera calle a la izquierda. 2 Coja la segunda calle a la derecha. 3 Siga todo derecho. 4 Siga hasta el final de esta calle, y doble a la derecha.

4.2 1 La Catedral. 2 El Banco de España 3 La Oficina de Turismo. 4 La Aduana. 5 La Plaza de Toros.

4.3 1 Lleno de súper, por favor. 2 treinta y cinco litros de súper, p.f. 3 ¿Quiere comprobar el aceite, p.f.? 4 ¿Quiere comprobar la presión, p.f.?

4.4 1 Mi coche no quiere arrancar. 2 El contacto no funciona. 3 ¿Puede mandar un mecánico, p.f.? 4 ¿Cuánto tiempo tardará?

4.5 Me duele el estómago y tengo diarrea./Desde hace una semana./Muchas gracias, adiós.

4.6 ¿Puede darme algo para las picaduras de insecto?/Quiero un paquete de esparadrapos y unas pastillas para la garganta, p.f.

5.1 1 Quiero una habitación doble. 2 . . . sencilla. 3 . . . con ducha. 4 . . . con baño. 5 . . . con dos camas.

5.2 Buenas tardes, he reservado una habitación./Me llamo . . ./Está en el coche./Muchas gracias.

5.3 ¿Tiene una habitación?/No, sólo con ducha./¿Cuánto es una habitación con baño?/Lo siento, es demasiado caro.

5.4 Buenas tardes. ¿Hay sitio, por favor?/Somos cuatro y tenemos una caravana./Una semana.

5.5 1 ¿Hay piscina? 2 ¿ . . . duchas calientes? 3 ¿ . . . supermercado? 4 ¿ . . . restaurante? 5 ¿ . . . Correos?

5.6 1 No funcionan las duchas calientes. 2 No funcionan los retretes. 3 No funciona la electricidad. 4 No funciona el grifo. 5 No funciona el agua potable.

5.7 (choice of menus)

5.8 De primero, los mejillones./Pues, voy a tomar la sopa de pescado./De segundo, la merluza al horno./Entonces. ¿hay filete de lenguado?/Una naranja, por favor./Vale. Un plátano, por favor.

6.1 Me gusta el tenis y la natación./No, no me gusta nada./Sí, pero prefiero el tenis.

6.2 Luisa: Me gusta el tenis, el baloncesto, el voleibol, y el golf. Juan: Me gusta la natación, la vela, el windsurf y la pesca.

6.3 (a) Dos entradas, por favor./Son doscientas cincuenta pesetas./¿A qué hora están abiertas?/Se abren a las tres de la tarde. (b) Dos entradas, por favor./Son ciento cincuenta pesetas./¿A qué hora se cierra?/Se cierra a las ocho.

6.4 1 (d). 2 (e). 3 (b). 4 (a). 5 (c).

6.5 2 ¿Conoce usted a Conchita, una amiga de mi esposa? 3 ¿Sabe jugar al ajedrez? 4 ¿Sabe usted cuándo se termina la reunión? 5 Sé que a mi esposa le gustaría mucho conocerle.

6.6 (personal preferences).

6.7 1 Art Exhibition. 2 Delgado is a painter; Teresa del Sol is a ceramist. 3 Open from Monday to Saturday. 4 From 6 pm to 8 pm. 5 10, Santa Catalina Street.

6.8 1 ¿Quedan localidades para la función de esta noche? 2 ¿Qué precio tienen las localidades? 3 Quisiera dos entradas, por favor. 4 ¿Cuánto es, por favor? 5 ¿A qué hora empieza el espectáculo?

7.1 Me levanto a las siete y media./Me desayuno./Salgo a las nueve y voy en autobús a mi oficina./Sí, vuelvo a casa a mediodía para almorzar. Después, voy de compras y vuelvo a la oficina por la tarde.

7.2 Me levanté a las siete y media./Me desayuné./Salí a las nueve y fui en autobús a mi oficina./Volví a casa a mediodía para almorzar. Después fui de compras, y entonces volví a la oficina por la tarde.

7.3 Dígame./Me gustaría mucho. ¿A qué hora vendré? Sí, sé donde vives y cogeré un taxi.

7.4 Estudiaba el español./Vivía en la Calle de Serrano con una familia española./Sí, había una hija./Se llamaba Mari-Carmen y tenía veintitrés años./Salía con unos amigos, o me quedaba en casa y leía, o miraba la televisión./Sí, me gustaba mucho. Lo pasaba muy bien.

7.5 Fue . . . estaba . . . tenía . . . salió . . . se dio . . . tenía . . . buscó.

TOPIC VOCABULARIES

English–Spanish topic vocabularies

Numbers 0–100

0	cero						
1	uno/una	11	once	21	veintiuno	31	treinta y uno
2	dos	12	doce	22	veintidós	32	treinta y dos,
3	tres	13	trece	23	veintitrés		etc
4	cuatro	14	catorce	24	veinticuatro	40	cuarenta
5	cinco	15	quince	25	veinticinco	50	cincuenta
6	seis	16	dieciséis	26	veintiséis	60	sesenta
7	siete	17	diecisiete	27	veintisiete	70	setenta
8	ocho	18	dieciocho	28	veintiocho	80	ochenta
9	nueve	19	diecinueve	29	veintinueve	90	noventa
10	diez	20	veinte	30	treinta	100	cien, ciento

Numbers 101–1000

101	ciento uno	500	quinientos/as	first	primero/a
150	ciento cincuenta	600	seiscientos/as	second	segundo/a
200	doscientos/as	700	setecientos/as	third	tercero/a
250	doscientos cincuenta	800	ochocientos/as	fourth	cuarto/a
300	trescientos/as	900	novecientos/as	fifth	quinto/a
400	cuatrocientos/as	1000	mil	sixth	sexto/a
				seventh	séptimo/a
1,500	mil quinientosas	ground floor	planta baja	eighth	octavo/a
2,000	dos mil	1st floor	primer piso	ninth	noveno/a
20,000	veinte mil	3rd floor	tercer piso	tenth	décimo/a
7,300	siete mil trescientos				

Days of the week (los días de la semana)

Monday	lunes	Friday	viernes
Tuesday	martes	Saturday	sábado
Wednesday	miércoles	Sunday	domingo
Thursday	jueves		

The day (el día)

morning	la mañana
afternoon	la tarde
evening	la tarde
night	la noche

The seasons (las temporadas)

Spring	la primavera
Summer	el verano
Autumn	el otoño
Winter	el invierno

Friday the 2nd February	viernes, dos de febrero
Last week/next month	la semana pasada/el próximo mes
Tomorrow, yesterday	mañana, ayer

TOPIC VOCABULARIES

Professions

accountant	contable	housewife	ama de casa
architect	arquitecto	journalist	periodista
businessman	hombre de negocios	lawyer	abogado
businesswoman	mujer de negocios	manager	director/gerente
civil servant	funcionaro	nurse	enfermero/a
computer operator	operario/a de computadoras	plumber	fontanero/a
		policeman	policía
dentist	dentista	salesman	representante
designer	diseñador/ora	secretary	secretaria
doctor	médico	shop assistant	dependiente/a
employee	empleado/a	social worker	asistente social
engineer	ingeniero	teacher	profesor/ora
farmer	agricultor	technician	técnico
electrician	electricista	unemployed	desempleado/a

Clothes (la ropa) and accessories

. . . for women	. . . para mujeres
. . . for men	. . . para hombres
. . . for children	. . . para jóvenes
. . . for babies	. . . para niños
bag	el bolso
belt	el cinturón
blouse	la blusa
bra	el sujetador
briefs/pants	los calzoncillos
coat	el abrigo
dress	el vestido
gloves	los guantes
handkerchief	el pañuelo
hat	el sombrero
jacket	la chaqueta
jeans	los vaqueros
jumper	el jersey
raincoat	el impermeable
sleeves	las manchas
scarf	la bufanda
(head)scarf	el pañuelo de cabeza
shirt	la camisa
skirt	la falda
shorts	los pantalones cortos
socks	los calcetines
stockings	las medias
suit	el traje
sweater	el suéter
swimming costume	el traje de baño
tights	el panty
trousers	los pantalones
t-shirt	la camiseta

Shoes

boots	las botas
sandals	las sandalias
shoes	los zapatos
slippers	las zapatillas

Colours

colour	el color
black	negro/a
blue	azul
brown	marrón
green	verde
grey	gris
red	rojo/a
white	blanco/a
yellow	amarillo/a
dark, light	oscuro/a/, claro/a

Materials

acrylic	el acrílico
cotton	el algodón
denim	el dril
leather	el cuero
nylon	el nilón
silk	la seda
suede	el ante
velvet	el terciopelo
wool	la lana

Note: You say: una falda **de** seda (= a skirt made of silk), and pantalones gris**es**, negr**os** etc.; camisetas blanc**as**

TOPIC VOCABULARIES

Pharmaceutical items, etc

aspirins	les aspirinas
bandage	la venda
contraceptive pill	la píldora
cotton-wool	el algodón
insect repellent	el repelente para insectos
pastilles (throat)	las pastillas
pill, tablet	el comprimido
sleeping-pill	el somnífero
sticking-plaster	el esparadrapo

Toiletries and other items

baby food	el alimento para bebé
comb	la peine
condoms	los condones
contraceptives	los anticonceptivos
dummy	el chupete
lipstick	el lápiz de labios
nappies	los pañales
perfume	el perfume
razor-blades	las hojas de afeitar
sanitary towels	las compresas
shampoo	el champú
shaving-cream	la crema bronceadora
soap	el jabón
sun-glasses	las gafas de sol
sun-tan cream	la crema bronceadora
tampons	los tampones
tissues	los pañuelos de papel
toilet-paper	el papel higiénico
toothbrush	el cepillo de dientes
toothpaste	la pasta de dientes

Food shops

baker's	la panadería
butcher's	la carnicería
cake shop	la pastelería
confectioner's	la confisería
dairy	la lechería
delicatessen	la mantequería
fishmonger's	la pescadería
fruit shop	la frutería
greengrocer's	la verdulería
grocer's	la tienda de alimentación, comestibles
market	el mercado
supermarket	el supermercado
wine merchant's	la tienda de vinos, la bodega

Tobacconist (el estanco)

cigar	el puro
cigarette	el cigarrillo
matches	los fósforos, las cerillas
newspaper	el periódico
magazine	la revista
postcard	la (tarjeta) postal
stamp	el sello
tobacco	el tabaco
(Virginian, black)	rubio, negro

Shops (las tiendas) and departments

bank	el banco
bookshop	la librería
camping equipment	el equipo de camping
chemist's	la farmacia
clothes shop	la tienda de ropa
cosmetics etc	la perfumería
dry cleaner's	la tintorería
hairdresser's	la peluquería
household (cleaning)	la droguería
ironmonger	la ferretería
news-stand	el quiosco
post-office	el correos
shoe-shop	la zapatería
stationer's	la papelería
tobacconist's	el estanco
toyshop	la juguetería

Fish (el pescado), Shellfish (los mariscos)

anchovy	la anchoa
bass	la lubina
bream	el besugo
clams	las almejas
cod	el bacalao
crab	el cangrejo
crayfish	los langostinos
hake	la merluza
lobster	la langosta
mussels	los mejillones
octopus	el pulpo
prawns	las gambas
red mullet	el salmonete
salmon	el salmón
sardine	la sardina
skate	la raya
sole	el lenguado
squid	los calamares
trout	la trucha
tuna	el atún

TOPIC VOCABULARIES

Fruit (la fruta)

apple	la manzana
apricot	el albaricoque
banana	el plátano
cherry	las cereza
dates	los dátiles
grapes	las uvas
fig	el higo
lemon	el limón
melon	el melón
orange	la naranja
nuts	las avellanas
peach	el melocotón
pear	la pera
pineapple	la piña
plum	la ciruela
raspberry	la frambuesa
strawberry	la fresa
watermelon	la sandia

Vegetables (las verduras)

artichoke	la alcachofa
asparagus	los espárragos
beans (broad)	las habas
beans (French)	los frijoles
cabbage	la berza
carrots	las zanahorias
cauliflower	la coliflor
garlic	el ajo
lettuce	la lechuga
mushroom	el champiñon
onion	la cebolla
olives	las aceitunas
pepper (sweet)	el pimiento
peas (chick)	los garbanzos
peas (green)	los guisantes
potato	la patata
salad	la ensalada
tomato	el tomate

Meat (la carne), Poultry (las aves)

beef	la carne de vaca
chicken	el pollo
ham	el jamón
lamb	el cordero
pork	el cerdo
rabbit	el conejo
sausage	el salchichón
sausages	las salchichas
veal	la ternera

Bread, etc.

bread, loaf	el pan
bread-roll	el panecillo
cake, pastry	el pastel
doughnut	el donut; el churro
tart, cake	la tarta, la torta

Groceries

biscuits	los bizcochos, las galletas
butter	la mantequilla
cheese	el queso
coffee	el café
eggs	los huevos
flour	la harina
milk	la leche
margarine	la margarina
oil	el aceite
pasta	la pasta
pepper	la pimienta
rice	el arroz
salt	la sal
sugar	el azúcar
tea	el té
vinegar	el vinagre

Parts of the car

battery	la bateria
brake(s)	el freno, los frenos
carburettor	el carburador
clutch	el embrague
engine	el motor
exhaust	el tubo de escape
fan-belt	la correa de ventilador
headlight	el faro
ignition	el contacto
indicator	el intermitente
wheel	la rueda
windscreen	el parabrisas
wipers	los limpiaparabrisas

Parts of the body

ankle	el tobillo
arm	el brazo
back	la espalda
blood	el sangre
bone	el hueso
chest	el pecho
ear	la oreja
elbow	el codo
eye	el ojo
face	la cara
finger	el dedo
foot	el pie
hair	los cabellos

TOPIC VOCABULARIES

hand	la mano
head	la cabeza
heart	el corazón
knee	la rodilla
leg	la pierna
lung	el pulmón
mouth	la boca
muscle	el músculo
nose	la nariz
rib	la costilla
shoulder	el hombro
skin	la piel
stomach	el estómago
throat	la garganta
thumb	el pulgar
tooth	el diente
toe	el dedo de pie
wrist	la muñeca

Places to visit and natural features

bridge	el puente
building	el edificio
castle	el castillo, el alcázar
cathedral	la catedral
church	la iglesia
cloister	el claustro
house	la casa
monastery	el monasterio
mosque	la mezquita
museum	el museo
palace	el palacio
wall	el muro
cave	la cueva
hill	la colina
island	la isla
lake	el lago
mountain	la montaña
mountain-range	la sierra
river	el río
sea	el mar
valley	el valle

Souvenirs (los recuerdos)

bull	el toro
castanets	las castañuelas
doll	la muñeca
fan	el abanico
necklace	el collar
pottery	la cerámica
el botijo	pottery jug
el pórron	glass wine container with long spout

Sports and games

archery	el tiro con arco
athletics	el atletismo
basketball	el baloncesto
cards	las cartas
chess	el ajedrez
cycling	el ciclismo
fishing	la pesca
football	el fútbol
golf	el golf
horse-riding	la equitación
judo	el yudo
jogging	el footing
rowing	el remo
sailing	la vela
shooting	la caza
swimming	la natación
tennis	el tenis
windsurfing	el windsurf
volleyball	el voleibol

Sports equipment

Where can I hire . . .	¿Dónde puedo alquilar . . .?
I'd like to hire . . .	Quiero alquilar . . .
a racket	una raqueta
some balls	unas pelotas
deck-chair	una silla de lona
fishing-rod	una caña
fishing-net	una red
sunshade	una sombrilla
golf-clubs	unos palos
ski-boots	unas botas de ski
ski-sticks	unos bastones
skis	unos esquís
canoe	una canoa
dinghy	un bote, un barca
sailing-boat	un velero, una barca de vela
sailboard	un windsurf
wetsuit	un traje de goma

championship	el campeonato
game	el juego
match, game	el partido
round of golf	una vuelta
stadium	el estadio
swimming-pool	la piscina
tennis court	la pista de tenis
tournament	el torneo
track, course	la pista

VOCABULARY

Spanish–English Vocabulary

Note: the letters **ch**, **ll** and **ñ** are counted as individual letters in Spanish and words beginning with these combinations are listed after **c**, **l** and **n** respectively.

a to, at
abierto/a open
abridor *m.* bottle-opener
abrir to open
abuelo, abuela grandfather, grandmother.
acabar to finish
accidente *m.* accident
aceite *m.* oil
aceituna *f.* olive
acrílico *m.* acrylic
acuerdo: de - agreed, I agree
adiós goodbye
aduana *f.* customs
aeropuerto *m.* airport
afición *f.* hobby
agencia *(f)* **de viajes** travel-agency
agradable pleasant
agua water: - **potable** drinking-water; - **mineral** mineral water
agujero *m.* hole
ahora now; - **mismo** this very moment
ajedrez *m.* chess
ajo *m.* garlic
albergue *(m)* **de juventud** youth hostel
albóndigas *f.pl.* meat-balls
alcázar *m.* Moorish castle
alegre happy
alérgico allergic
algo something; ¿ - **más?** anything else?
algodón *m.* cotton
algún, alguno some, any
almacén *m.* store; **los grandes almacenes** department store
almeja *f.* clam
almorzar to have lunch
almuerzo *m.* lunch
alquilar to hire
alquiler *(m)* **de coches** car-rental
alto/a tall, high
amable kind, nice
ambulancia *(f)* ambulance
amigo *m.* **amiga** *f.* friend
ancho/a wide
anchoa *f.* anchovy
andar to walk; **andando** walking
andén *m.* platform
anticiclón *m.* anticyclone
año *m.* year

aparatos eléctricos *m.pl.* electric appliances
aparcamiento *m.* parking space, car-park
aparcar to park
apellido *m.* surname
aquí here
arrancar to start (of car)
arreglar to fix, mend
artículo *m.* article
asiento *m.* seat
autobús *m.* bus
autocar *m.* coach
autopista *f.* motorway
avería *f.* breakdown
averiado broken (down)
avión *m.* aeroplane
ayer yesterday
ayudar to help
ayuntamiento *m.* town-hall
azúcar *m.* sugar
azul blue

bajar to go down, get down
bajo/a low, short; under
bailar to dance
balcón *m.* balcony
banco *m.* bank
bañarse to bathe
baño *m.* bathroom; bath
bar *m.* bar
barato/a cheap
barca *(f)* **de vela** sailing-boat
barco *m.* ship
barra *f.* bar, counter (inside bar)
bastante quite; enough
batido *m.* milkshake
beber to drink
bebida *m.* drink
biblioteca *f.* library
bien well
billete *m.* bank-note; ticket; - **de ida y vuelta** return
bistec *m.* steak
blanco/a white
boca *f.* mouth
bocadillo *m.* sandwich
bodega *f.* wine-cellar
bolso *m.* handbag

VOCABULARY

bonito/a pretty
borrasca f. low-pressure area
botella f. bottle
buen, bueno/a good, well; buenos días good morning; buenas tardes good afternoon
buscar to look for

cabeza f. head
cabina telefónica f. telephone box
cada each
café m. coffee; - con leche white coffee; - sólo black coffee
cafetería f. café
caja f. cash desk; box
cala f. cove
calamar m. squid
caliente hot
calor m. heat; tengo - I am hot
calle f. street
cama f. bed; - matrimonial double bed
cámara f. camera
camarero m. waiter
cambiar to change
cambio m. change; currency exchange
camino m. way, road
camión m. lorry
camisa f. shirt
camiseta f. t-shirt
camping m. campsite
caravana f. caravan
carne f. meat
carnet (m) de identidad identity card
carnicería f. butcher's shop
caro/a expensive
carretera f. road, highway
carta f. menu; letter
cartelera f. entertainments page
casa f. house
casado/a married
castillo m. castle
catedral f. cathedral
caza f. shooting, hunting
ceda el paso give way
cena f. dinner, supper
cenar to have dinner
centro m. centre; - ciudad city centre
cepillo (m) de dientes toothbrush
cerca (de) near to
cercano near
cerdo m. pork
cerilla f. match
cerrado/a shut

cerrar to shut
cerveza f. beer
cheque (m) de viaje traveller's cheque
cielo m. sky
cigarrillo m. cigarette
cine m. cinema
cinturón m. de seguridad seat-belt
circo m. circus
cita f. appointment
ciudad f. city
claro certainly, of course; light (adj)
cobro revertido m. reverse charges call
coche m. car; coach (of train) - cama sleeping-car; - litera couchette
cocina f. kitchen
coger to take, catch
coja take (from coger)
colegio m. school
color m. colour
collar m. necklace
comedor m. dining-room
comer to eat
comida f. meal, lunch
como how, as, like
¿cómo? how? what?
cómodo/a comfortable
completo/a full
comprar to buy
comprender to understand
compresa f. sanitary towel
comprimido m. pill
computadora f. computer
con with
conejo m. rabbit
conocer to know (person or place)
consigna f. left luggage
controlar to check
coñac m. brandy
copa f. cup; tomar una - to have a drink
correos post office
correspondencia f. connection (train)
corrida f. bullfight
cordero m. lamb
corriente m. current (electric)
corto/a short
costa f. coast
costar to cost
crédito m. credit; tarjeta de - credit card; carta de - letter of credit
crema (f) de tomate tomato soup
cruce m. crossroads
cruzar to cross; cruzca cross over
¿cuál? which?

VOCABULARY

¿cuál? which?

¿cuándo? when?

¿cuánto(s), cuánta(s)? how much? how many?

cuarto *m.* room; - de dormir bedroom; - de estar living-room ; - de baño bathroom

cuarto *m.* quarter; - de hora quarter of an hour; - de kilo quarter of a kilo

cubierto *m.* cover-charge; overcast (adj)

cubo *(m)* de basura rubbish-bin

cuchara *f.* spoon -da spoonful

cuchillo *m.* knife

cuenta *f.* bill; account; darse - de to realise

cuesta, cuestan it costs, they cost (from costar)

cueva *f.* cave

¡cuidado! careful!

champiñon *m.* mushroom

champú *m.* shampoo

chaqueta *f.* jacket

chica *f.* girl

chico *m.* boy

chocolate *m.* chocolate

choque *m.* collision

chorizo *m.* spicy sausage

chubasco *m.* shower

chuleta *f.* cup

dar to give; dame, deme give me

deber to owe

decir to say

dejar to leave

delante (de) in front (of)

delgado/a slim, thin

demasiado too, too much

deme give me (from dar)

dentista *m/f.* dentist

dentro (de) within

dependiente/a *m/f.* shop assistant

deporte *m.* sport

derecha *f.* right; a la - on/to the right

derecho: todo straight ahead

desayuno *m.* breakfast

descuento *m.* discount

desde since

desear to want

despacho *m.* office; - de billetes ticket-office

despacio: ir más – to slow down

despejado clear (sky)

después (de) afterwards, after

destino *m.* destination

desviación *f.* diversion

detrás (de) behind

devuelve cambio gives change (from devolver to give back)

día *m.* day

diabético/a diabetic

diarrea *f.* diarrhoea

diccionario *m.* dictionary

diente *m.* tooth; - de ajo clove of garlic

¡diga!¡ ¡dígame! hello! (on telephone)

dinero *m.* money

dirección *f.* direction; -única one-way street; address

directo direct

disco *m.* record, disc

discoteca *f.* discotheque

divertirse to enjoy oneself

doblar to turn; doble a la derecha turn right

doble double

docena *f.* dozen

doctor *m.* doctor

doler to hurt, have a pain

domicilio *m.* residence

domingo Sunday

¿dónde? where?

dormir to sleep

ducha *f.* shower

duro *m.* 5-peseta coin

edificio *m.* building

el the (masc)

él, ella, he, she; him, her

ellos, ellas they; them

electricidad *f.* electricity

embarazada pregnant

empezar to begin

empresa *f.* company, firm

empujar to push

en in, on

encantar to delight

encender to light

encontrar to meet

enfermera *f.* nurse

enfermo/a ill

enfrente (de) opposite

ensaimada *f.* roll

ensalada *f.* salad

enseñar to show

entender to understand

entonces well, then

VOCABULARY

entrada *f.* entrance; entrance-ticket; hors d'oeuvres

entregar to hand over; **entrega de equipajes** baggage in

enviar to send

equipaje *m.* luggage

equipo *m.* team

equitación *f.* riding

es he, she, it is; you are (formal)

escalera *f.* staircase

escaparse to run away

escocés, escocesa Scottish

escuchar to listen

ese, esa that; **esos, esas** those; **eso** (neuter) that (pronoun)

eso that; **a eso de** about

español, española Spanish

esparadrapo *m.* sticking-plaster

espárragos *m.pl.* asparagus

esposa *f.* wife

esquí *m.* ski; skiing - **acuático** waterskiing

esquina *f.* corner

esta this; **estas** these (fem); **ésta** this (one); **éstas** these (ones)

estación *f.* station, - **de ferrocarril** railway station, - **de servicio** service station. - **de autobuses** bus station

estacionamiento *m.* parking

estadio *m.* stadium

estanco *m.* tobacconist's

estar to be

estatua *f.* statue

este this, **estos** these (masc); **éste** this (one), **éstos** these (ones)

estilo *m.* style

esto (*neuter*) this (one) (pronoun)

estómago *m.* stomach

estrecho/a narrow, tight

estudiante *m/f.* student

estupendo/a great!

examen *m.* examination

excursión *f.* excursion

exposición *f.* exhibition

expreso *m.* express train

extranjero/a foreign; **al -** abroad

fábrica *f.* factory

falda *f.* skirt

farmacia *f.* chemist's, pharmacy

fecha *f.* date

ferretería *f.* hardware shop

ferrocarril *m.* railway

festivos: días - public holidays

ficha *f.* form

fideos *m.pl.* pasta (vermicelli etc)

fiebre *f.* fever; - **del heno** hay fever

fiesta *f.* festival, party

fila *f.* row

filete *m.* fillet

final: al - at the end

firma *f.* signature

firmar to sign

flan *m.* caramel custard

flauta *f.* flute

folleto *m.* brochure

formulario *m.* form

foto *f.* photograph

fresa *f.* strawberry

fresco/a cool

frío/a cool

frito/a fried

fruta *f.* fruit

frutería *f.* fruit shop

fumar to smoke; **(no) fumador;** (non) smoker

funcionar to work; **no funciona** it is not working

funcionario/a civil servant

fútbol *m.* football

gafas *f.pl.* glasses; - **de sol** sunglasses

galés, galesa Welsh

galleta *f.* biscuit

gamba *f.* prawn

ganas: tener - de to want to

garaje *m.* garage

gas: con - fizzy; **sin -** still (of drinks)

gaseosa *f.* fizzy lemonade

gasóleo *m.* diesel

gasolina *f.* petrol

gasolinera *f.* petrol station

gazpacho *m.* cold soup

gente *f.* people

gordo/a fat

gracias thank you

gramo *m.* gramme

grande big; **los grandes almacenes** department store(s)

grave serious

grifo *m.* tap

gripe *f.* influenza

gris grey

guapo/a handsome, pretty

guía *f.* guide-book; *m/f.* guide

guisantes *m.pl.* peas

VOCABULARY

guitarra *f.* guitar
gustar to like; **me gusta** I like

habitación *f.* room; **- doble** double room;
   - individual/sencilla single room
hablar to speak
hacer to do; to make; **hace dos años** two
   years ago; **hace sol** it is sunny; **hace
   frío/calor** it is cold/hot
hacia towards
hambre *m.* hunger; **tengo -** I am hungry
hamburguesa *f.* hamburger
hasta until
hay there is, there are; **- que** one must
helado *m.* ice-cream
hermano/a *m/f.* brother/sister
herido/a hurt
hielo *m.* ice
hígado *m.* liver
hijo/a *m/f.* son/daughter
hoguera *f.* bonfire
hola hello
hombre *m.* man
hora *f.* hour, time
horario *m.* timetable
hospital *m.* hospital
hostal *m.* family hotel
hotel *m.* hotel
hoy today
huevo *m.* egg

ida single (ticket) - **y vuelta** return
idioma *m.* language
iglesia *f.* church
importa: no - it doesn't matter
incluido/a included
información *f.* information
ingeniero *m.* engineer
inglés, inglesa English
insolación *f.* sunstroke
interesar to interest; **-se** to be interested
   (in)
invierno *m.* Winter
ir to go; **-se** to go away, leave
isla *f.* island
izquierda *f.* left; **a la -** on/to the left

jabón *m.* soap
jamón *m.* ham
jardín *m.* garden
jerez *m.* sherry
jersey *m.* pullover
juego *m.* game

jueves *m.* Thursday
jugar to play (game)
juguetería *f.* toyshop

kilo *m.* kilogramme
kilómetro *m.* kilometre

la, las the (feminine)
lado *m.* side; **al otro -** on the other side;
   al - de beside
lana *f.* wool
largo/a long
lástima *f.* : **¡Qué - !** What a pity!
lata *f.* tin
lávabo *m.* basin
lavar to wash
leche *f.* milk
lechería *f.* dairy
leer to read
legumbres *f.pl.* pulses
lejos far; **- de** far from
lenguado *m.* sole
lentillas *f.pl.* contact lenses
lento slowly
levantarse to get up
libra *f.* pound
libre free, vacant
librería *f.* bookshop
libro *m.* book
limón *m.* lemon
limonada *f.* lemonade
linea *f.* line
liquidación *f.* clearance sale
lista *f.* list; **- de vinos** wine-list
litro *m.* litre
localidad *f.* seat, ticket
lugar *m.* place
lunes *m.* Monday

llamar to call, telephone; **-se** to be
   called
llave *f.* key
llegadas *f.pl.* arrivals
llegar to arrive
llenar to fill in; fill up
lleno/a full
llevar to buy, to take; to wear
llover to rain; **llueve** it is raining
lluvia *f.* rain

macarrones *m.* macaroni
madre *f.* mother
maduro/a ripe

VOCABULARY

mal, malo/a bad
maleta f. suitcase
manchego/a from La Mancha
mandar to send
mantequilla f. butter
manzana f. apple
mañana f. morning; tomorrow; - por la - tomorrow morning
mapa m. map
mar m/f. sea; - arbolada very rough sea
maravilloso/a wonderful
marca f. make (of car)
marcar to dial (a number)
mareado/a faint, dizzy
marido m. husband
mariscos m.pl. shellfish
martes m. Tuesday
más more
matrícula f. number (registration)
me me
mecánico m. mechanic
medio/a half; mediodía midday; media-noche midnight; y media half past
medias f.pl. stockings
médico m. doctor
mejillones m.pl. mussels
mejorarse to get better
melocotón m. peach
menos less
menú m. fixed price meal
mercado m. market
merluza f. hake
merienda f. snack
mermelada f. jam
mes m. month
mesa f. table
meter to put, insert
metro m. metro, underground; metre
mezquita f. mosque
mi, mis my
mí me (emphatic)
miércoles m. Wednesday
minuto m. minute
mirar to watch, look
mismo/a same
moderno/a modern
monasterio m. monastery
moneda f. coin, change
monumento m. monument
mostrar to show
mucho much; muchísimo very much
muebles m.pl. furniture
mujer f. woman

multa f. fine
museo m. museum
muy very

nacionalidid f. nationality
nada nothing; de - you're welcome; - más no more, that's all
nadar to swim
naranja f. orange
naranjada f. orangeade
nata f. cream
natación f. swimming
necesitar to need
negocios: de - on business
negro black
neumático m. tyre
niebla f. fog
nieve f. snow
niña f. little girl
niño m. child; little boy
ningún, ninguno/a none, not any
no no, not
noche f. night
nombre m. name
normal 2-star (petrol)
norte m. north
nosotros we, us
nube f. cloud
nublado, nuboso m. cloudy
nuevo/a new
número m. number; size (of shoe)

obra f. work; obras roadworks
ocupado occupied
oeste m. west
oficina f. office
ojo m. eye
olvidarse to forget
oscuro/a dark
otro/a other, another
oye listen (from oír to listen)

padre m. father; -s parents
pagar to pay
país m. country
palacio m. palace
pan m. bread
panadería f. baker's
panecillo m. bread-roll
pantalones m.pl. trousers
papel m. paper; -es de seguro insurance papers

VOCABULARY

papelería f. stationer's
paquete m. packet
par m. pair
para to, for
parada f. bus-stop
parar to stop
parecer to seem; me parece que I think
  that
parque m. park
partido m. match (football)
pasado/a previous, last; la semana
  pasada last week
pasaporte m. passport
pasar to spend (time); to pass; to
  happen
pasear to go for a walk
paseo m. walk; broad avenue
paso m. way
pasta (f) de dientes toothpaste
pastel m. pastry, cake
pastelería f. cake shop
pastilla f. pastille
patata f. potato
peaje m. toll
peatones m.pl. pedestrians
película f. film (in cinema, etc)
peligro m. danger
pelo m. hair
peluquería f. hairdresser's
pensar to think
pensión f. boarding-house; board; -
  completa full board; - media half
  board
pequeño/a small
pera f. pear
perdón pardon, excuse me
perfume m. perfume
perfumería f. cosmetics shop
periódico m. newspaper
periodista m/f. journalist
permiso (m). de conducir driving
  licence
persona f. person
pesca f. fishing
pescadería f. fishmonger's
pescado m. fish
peseta f. peseta (unit of currency)
picadura f. sting
picar to sting
pie m. foot; a - on foot
pila f. battery
píldora f. contraceptive pill
pimienta f. pepper

pimiento m. pepper (green etc)
pinchazo m. puncture
pintura f. painting
piscina f. swimming-pool
piso m. floor (storey); flat (apartment)
pista f. track, court; - de tenis tennis-
  court
plano m. plan, map
planta (f) baja ground floor
plátano m. banana
plato m. plate, dish; - combinado meal
  on one plate
playa f. beach
plaza f. square; seat; - de toros bullring;
  plazas libres seats vacant
plomo m. lead
poco little, a little
poder to be able
policía f. police; m. policeman
pollo m. chicken
poner to put; póngame give me; to show
  (a film)
por for, through, during, along; - favor
  please; - aquí this way, ¿por qué?
  why?
porque because
porrón m. glass wine container
postal f. postcard
postre m. dessert
practicar to practise
precio m. price
preferir to prefer
prefijo m. area code (telephone)
preocuparse to worry
presentar to introduce
presión f. pressure
primavera f. Spring
primer, primero/a first
primo m., prima f. cousin
principos: a - de at the beginning (of)
probador m. fitting-room
probarse to try on
profesor m., profesora f. teacher
profundo/a deep
prohibido forbidden
pronóstico m. forecast
propina f. tip
próximo/a next
puede: ¿se puede? can one?
puente m. bridge
puerta f. door
puerto m. port
puesto (m) de socorro first aid post

90

VOCABULARY

que what, that, than; ¿qué? what? which? how?; ¿qué tal? how are you? (informal)
quedar to keep, be left; quedarse to stay, remain
querer to want; quiero I want
queso *m.* cheese
¿quién? who?
quiosco *m.* news-stand
quisiera I should'like
quizás perhaps

rabajas *f.pl.* bargains
ración *f.* portion
rápido *m.* fast train
rato: un - a while
recado *m.* message
recepción *f.* reception
receta *f.* prescription
recogida *(f.)* de equipajes baggage collection
reducción *f.* reduction
refresco *m.* soft drink
reloj *m.* watch, clock
reparar to repair
reserva *f.* reservation
reservar to reserve
resfriado *m.* cold, catarrh
residencia *f.* guest-house
respirar to breathe
restaurante *m.* restaurant
resto *m.* remainder
retraso *m.* delay
revista *f.* magazine
río *m.* river
robar to steal
roca *f.* rock
rodaja *f.* slice
rojo/a red
ropa *f.* clothes
rubio/a *m.* fair

sábado Saturday
saber to know
sacar to take out, get (tickets)
sacacorchos *m.* corkscrew
saco *(m.)* de dormir sleeping-bag
sal *f.* salt
sala *(f.)* de espera waiting room
salchichón *m.* sausage
salchichas *f.pl.* sausages
salida *f.* exit; salidas departures
salsa *(f.)* de tomate tomato sauce

sandwich *(m.)* caliente toasted sandwich
sangría *f.* red wine cup
secretaria *f.* secretary
seda *f.* silk
seguida: en - at once
seguir to follow, continue
segundo second; de - for the second course
seguro *m.* insurance; sure (adj)
sello *m.* stamp
semana *f.* week
sentar to fit, suit; -se to sit
sentirse to feel; lo siento I'm sorry
señor Mr., gentleman
señorita Miss, young lady
señora Mrs. lady
ser to be
serio serious
servicio *m.* service; -s toilets
sesión *(f.)* continua continuous performance
si if
sí yes
siempre always
¡siga! follow! (from seguir)
simpático/a nice, pleasant
sin without
sitio *m.* place, site
sobre above, over; - todo especially
sol *m.* sun; hace - it is sunny
sólo only; café - black coffee
soltero/a single (unmarried)
sombrero *m.* hat
somnífero *m.* sleeping-pill
sopa *f.* soup
su his, her, its, their; your
subir to go up, climb
suéter *m.* sweater
súper 4-star (petrol)
supermercado *m.* supermarket
suplemento *m.* surcharge
sur *m.* south

tabla *f.* a vela windsurfer
tacón *m.* heel
tal such; ¿qué tal? how are you?
talla *f.* size
taller mecánico *m.* workshop, garage
también also
tapas *f.pl.* appetizers
taquilla *f.* ticket window
tardar to delay, to take time
tarde *f.* afternoon, early evening; late

VOCABULARY

tarjeta *f.* card; - **postal** postcard; **tarjeta de crédito** credit card
tarta *f.* tart, cake
taxi *m.* taxi
taza *f.* cup
té *m.* tea
teatro *m.* theatre
teléfono *m.* telephone
televisor *m.* television
temperatura *f.* temperature
templado mild
temporal *m.* gale, storm
tenderse to lie down
tenedor *m.* fork
tener to have; **tengo hambre/sed** I am hungry/thirsty; **tengo veinte años** I am twenty years old
tenis *m.* tennis
terminar to finish; **terminado** finished
ternera *f.* veal
terraza *f.* terrace, balcony
tiempo *m.* weather
tienda *f.* shop - **(de campaña)** tent
tierra *f.* land
tinto *m.* red wine
tirita *f.* bandage
toalla *f.* towel; - **de baño** bathtowel
tocar to play (instrument)
todo all, every; everything; - **derecho** straight ahead
tomar to take; - **una copa** to have a drink
tomate *m.* tomato
tormenta *f.* thunderstorm
toro *m.* bull
tortilla *f.* omelette
tos *f.* cough
tostada *f.* toast
trabajar to work
trabajo *m.* work, job
traer to bring; **¡traiga!** bring!
traje *m.* suit; - **de baño** bathing costume
transbordo *m.* change
transeúnte *m.* passer-by
tren *m.* train; **-es de cercanías** local trains; **-es de largo recorrido** long-distance trains
triste sad
trozo *m.* piece
tú you (informal)
tu your (informal)
turismo *m.* tourism
turista *m/f.* tourist

último/a last
un, uno/una a; one; **unos/unas** some
usted/ustedes you (formal)

vacaciones *f.pl.* holidays; **de** - on holiday
vainilla *f.* vanilla
¡vale! OK!
valer to cost, to be worth
valor *m.* value
valle *f.* valley
vamos let's go
vaqueros *m.pl.* jeans
vaso *m.* glass
vendedor *m.*, **vendedora** *f.* sales assistant
venir to come; **¡venga!** come here!
venta *f.* sale; - **anticipada** advance sales
ventana *f.* window
ver to see; **a** - let's see
verano *m.* Summer
¿verdad? isn't it? aren't you? don't you?
verde green
verdulería *f.* greengrocer's
verduras *f.pl.* vegetables
vermut *m.* vermouth
vestido *m.* dress
vez *f.* time; **una** - once; **dos veces** twice
vía *f.* track, platform
viajar to travel
viaje *m.* journey
viejo/a old
viento *m.* wind
viernes *m.* Friday
vinagre *m.* vinegar
vino *m.* wine
visitar visit
vista *f.* view; - **del mar** sea view; **hasta la** - till we meet again
vivir to live
volver to return
vosotros you (plural)
vuelo *m.* flight
vuelta *f.* change; walk

y and
ya already
yo I

zapatería *f.* shoe-shop
zapatos *m.pl.* shoes
zumo *m.* juice